iPhone 12 Fo

The Complete User Guide Manual for Seniors,

Beginners and Kids

Derell Mathow

Table of Contents

Introduction

Are you new to iPhone 12 mini, iPhone 12, iPhone Pro, or iPhone 12 Pro max?

Or are you new totally to the iPhone world by trying to acquire any of the latest iPhone mobile or the previous version of iPhone 11 Pro Max, iPhone X, iPhone 8 plus, down to iPhone 6?

This book shows you new and exciting tips and in-depth tutorials you need to know about the new iPhone features and the iOS 14 user interface.

This guide is packed with top tips and in-depth tutorials. You'll uncover the exclusive features of this new iPhone, learn how to take incredible photos, learn how to start dark mode settings and customize your phone, discover how to use iOS 14 like a professional, how to create and use iPhone shortcuts and gestures, and its built-in apps, plus much more.

This book is updated with information on iOS 14, the newly released software in Fall of 2020 that runs on all iPhone device, dating back to the iPhone 6.

This book will help you navigate your device easily and effortlessly.

This book has information with clear, step-by-step information on the essentials information you would need on daily basis. It covers the basics of setting up an iPhone, backing up and restoring of data, setting up Face ID, email, screen recording, etc.

This books also covers;

- Overview of what the new iPhone features are,
- Upgrade to iOS 14
- iPhone 12 cameras and Voice mail
- Customizing iPhone
- Siri on your iPhone
- Backup and restore of data on iTunes, iCloud and Android
- iPhone Tips and Tricks
- Fix common iPhone problems

…and much more

If you looking for the most recent information on your iPhone, look no further than this book best suitable for beginners, dummies, seniors and kids.

Whenever you're ready to build your skills and become

the iPhone guru of your dream, this is the guide that offers the insight you need to increase your technical know-how.

Chapter 1

iPhone Setup

For some, the new iPhone would radically not be exactly like the prior iPhone model. And also, the iPhone setup procedure hasn't really changed. However, you may may go through the same procedure of setting up your new iPhone;

Let's have a look at how to setup your brand-new iPhone device the right way.

<u>Setup iPhone:</u>

With iPhone, if you're with an updated iPhone without **Face ID**, you'll discover that **Touch ID** is entirely gone.

(This means you'll maintain one face, instead of several.)

iPhone Setup: The Fundamentals

Re-download just the applications you'll need; which is vital. Several people have a lot of applications on their iPhone that they do not use; this is the big reason we recommend the execution of a new setup. Make use of the App Store application and be certain you're authorized into the Apple accounts. (Touch the tiny icon from the Updates-panel to find out which accounts you're logged on to.) Just download applications you have in the past half of a year.

Set up **Do Not Disturb** - If you're like other people, you're constantly getting *notifications, iMessages*, and other forms of alert on your iPhone. Create **DO NOT Disturb** in the *Configurations settings* (it's in the next section below *Notifications* and *Control Centre*). You'll need to regulate it for other events if you wouldn't want to be bothered.

Toggle *Alarm* to *On* and *Messages* when you wish to receive *Notifications*.

Note: Let some things through if there's an alert: Enable

Allow Calls From your Favourites and toggle *Repeated Calls* to *On.* iOS 14 also lets you switch on **Do Not Disturb** at night, which mutes all notifications as well as hides them through the lock screen, so you don't get distracted when you consider the phone to check on the time.

Auto Setup for iPhone

Secondly; *Auto Setup* lets you duplicate your **Apple ID** and home *Wi-Fi* configurations from another device, by just geting them close.

If the old *iPhone (or iPad)* was already operating previous version of iOS, putting simply the devices close to another, then follow the prompts notification to avoid having to enter your *Apple ID* and *Wi-Fi* passwords; this makes the initial iPhone work much better.

Restoring Data from back-up of old iPhone

You'll oftentimes be restoring your data from the old iPhone to your new iPhone. If that's so, you will then have to do either of these;

- be sure you add an up-to-date *backup.*

- use Apple's new *Auto-setup* features to truly get you started.

- The very first thing is as simple as likely to the *iCloud settings* on your *iPhone*, and taking a look at that, they're surely a recently available automated back-up. If not, do one yourself. Check out *Settings > Your Name > iCloud > iCloud Back-up* and tap **Backup Now**. Wait until it is done.

Setup Face ID

Face ID is a lot simpler to use than **Touch ID**, and it's better to create. Rather than having to unlocking and interacting with your iPhone with your fingerprints, independently, you simply can use the camera, and that's almost it. To *setup Face* **ID** on your iPhone, do this when prompted through the preliminary *iPhone setup*. (If you want to start over having a phone you setup previously, have a look at *Settings > Face ID & Passcode, and enter your password*, to start.)

- Establishing *Face ID* is comparable to the compass calibration your *iPhone* lets you do sometimes by using the *Map app*. Just instead of turning the iPhone around, you turn your face. You'll do two scans, and the iPhone could have your head stored in its Secure Enclave, inaccessible to anything, even to *iOS* itself (despite some clickbait "news" stories).

- Now, still, in *Settings/Configurations* > *Face ID & Passcode*, you can pick which features to use with *Face ID*, as everybody else did with *Touch ID*.

Create iPhone Email

- Enter your email accounts - You'll need to add your email accounts immediately. For Apple's Email app, tap *Configurations* > *Accounts & Passwords*, then tap *Add Accounts*. Choose your *email provider* and follow the steps to enter all of the knowledge required.

- Check email preview - Email enables you to start seeing the content material of an email without starting it. May as well be seen as a whole. Go to *Settings* > *Email* and tap on the *Preview button*.

Change your *configurations* to five lines and get more information from the *email messages* and never having to have them open up.

- Establish your default accounts - For reasons unknown, your *iOS Email settings* may be on default to a particular merchant account like *iCloud*. Tap *Configurations > Accounts & Passwords > Your email accounts name, and touch Accounts > Email*. Once you reach the end of the settings, you can tap on your selected email; this might open your address in new mails. That's also the location to add various other email addresses connected with your email account.

Advanced iPhone Email Tweaks

- *Swipe to Regulate Email* - It's a lot more helpful to be capable of swiping your electronic mails away instead of clicking through, and clicking on several links. Swipe to **Archive**, in order that once you swipe that path, you'll be capable of either quickly save a contact to your *Archive*. Or, in case your email accounts support swiping left like a default

Delete action, it'll provide a *Recycle icon.* Swipe left to *Tag* as *Read,* which is a wise way to slam through your electronic mails as you maintain these actions. This impacts your built-in Email application on Apple. Each third-party email customer can do things differently.

- Increase an *HTML* signature - An email signature can make you appear professional, so be sure to add an *HTML signature* to your email. If you've already got one on the desktop, duplicate and paste the code into contact and send to yourself.

- You can copy and paste it into a contact application (or whichever email supplier you prefer, if it facilitates it). Maybe it's as easy as wording formatting tags or as complicated as adding a company logo from a webserver. You need to use an *iOS application* to create one, too; however, they have a tendency to appear fairly basic.

- Manage *Calendars, iCloud, Communications* and more

- Place default *Calendar* alert - Calendar is fantastic

for alerting you of important occasions, but it's not at a convenient or leisure time. Establish the default timing on three types of occasions: *Birthdays, Events, and All-Day Events*, so you get reminders when they're helpful. Go to *Settings > Calendars*. Tap on *Default **Reminder*** and set your Birthday reminders to at least one day before, your *Event* to quarter-hour before (or an interval which makes even more sense to you), and All-Day Occasions on your day from the function (10 a.m.). You'll never miss an event again.

- *Background application refresh* - You'll need to be selective about which applications you want to work in the background, so check out the list in *Settings > General > Background App Refresh*. Toggle Background App Refresh to *ON*, then toggle *OFF* all of the applications you don't need having the ability to access anything in the background. When involved, toggle it *OFF* and discover if you're slowed down by any application that want to refresh when you release them. You'll need to allow background Refresh.

Chapter 2

iPhone 12 Overview

More than almost all years, there are a great number of features that are new on the iPhone 12. Apple has brought in the most common upgrades just like a *faster processor chip* and *improved digital camera*, but that is something we have arrived at expectedly. Along with all that, there is a *brand-new design, a brand-new OLED screen, a completely brand-new charging and accessories ecosystem with MagSafe, and, needless to say, 5G.*

It appears obvious that both Apple and its provider partners want to align to create this supercycle for improvements. All that brand-new features can be combined with both an increased cost ($829 for the low 64GB model) and discount rates, and heavily promoted service provider trade-in and installment programs. Amidst a pandemic-induced economic depression, maybe it's a hard market.

It's an easy task to recommend the default iPhone for the changing times if you want a new cell phone anyhow, but it's a lot more difficult to say whether all this brand-new features results in a thing that could compel you to upgrade sooner than you had planned.

iPhone 12 Pro Overview

It's a big year for the iPhone: Apple's iPhone 12 collection is completely re-designed and has four versions - the **iPhone 12 mini**, the **iPhone 12**, the **iPhone 12 Pro**, as well as the **iPhone 12 Pro Max** - at a variety of display sizes and cost points. Over the table, Apple's added *brand-new video features, a brand-new MagSafe charging program, the brand new A14 processor chip, and all the hype it could muster for 5G.*

It's obvious what differentiates the mini and Max iPhone 12s aside, but the two 6.1-inch choices at the center of the line are usually remarkably comparable. The iPhone 12 as well as the iPhone 12 Pro have the same fundamental design, virtually identical **OLED** screen, and the same processors and **5G** abilities. The Pro adds a supplementary telephoto camera zoom lens, a **LIDAR**

sensor, a bit more **RAM**, twice the mini storage, along with a shiny stainless frame. All that may set you back $999, around $200 more than a first iPhone 12 in the carrier-subsidized cost of $799.

Now, there are a few of you that are likely to spend the excess money because this is the shiny one. Generally, I would have the same option because I've arrived and accepted my weak points. But it's well worth diving directly into to see if the excess money will probably be worth it, specifically because the iPhone 12 right now comes with an *OLED screen*, this means the variations between the normal iPhone as well as the **Pro** are fundamentally very much minier than this past year when the normal model experienced a *lower-resolution LCD*.

So the true question for your **iPhone 12 Pro** is if the set of more functions justifies an approximately $200 cost bump from the typical iPhone 12. And when you're investing that a lot more, it could be worth it to hold back a time longer and invest another $100 on the **iPhone 12 Pro Max**, which has a larger display and a more substantial main digital camera sensor with an extremely intriguing brand-new *sensor-shift stabilization program* that could provide a large jump in display quality.

That results in the 12 Pro in a strange place, and really, I believe it boils down to just how much you may use the telephoto zoom lens or shoot family portrait photos during the night.

How to Screen Record on the iPhone 12

What to Know

- Initially, add it to the ***Control Center***. Tap *Settings > control center > scroll right down to Screen recording and tap the + (green plus) logo.*

- Swipe down to open up the *Control center*, tap the *Screen Record* icon. After a 3-2s delay, the recording will start.

- To stop recording, tap the *red status bar* at the very top left of your screen, then stop.

NB: This instruction below explains how to add the screen record substitute for the iPhone 12's Control Center in addition to how to begin and prevent screen recording.

How to Add Screen Record to Your iPhone 12

Before Recording your display on iPhone 12, you will need to add the choice to your Handle Center to get the controls very easily. Here's how exactly to add it.

1. On your iPhone 12, tap **Settings**.

2. Tap **Control center**.

3. Scroll right down to **Screen Recording**.

4. Touch the **+ (green plus) logo** close to it.

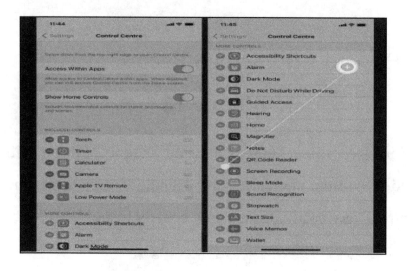

5. Screen Recording settings have been put into your **Control center**.

Screen Recording on iPhone 12

Recording your display screen on iPhone 12 is easy once you add the relevant substitute to your ***Control Center.***

1. On your iPhone, swipe down from your upper-right corner of the screen.

Tip: *You can do this through the lock screen or even whilst your iPhone 12 is unlocked.*

2. Tap the ***Display Record*** icon.

3. Wait for 3 seconds for the saving to begin.

4. You'll now be recording everything on your screen

and you can stop the recording.

5. To stop recording your screen, touch the *red status bar* at the very top left corner of the screen.

6. Tap ***Stop.***

7. The video is automatically saved to **Gallery**.

How to Screen Record with Sound on iPhone 12

By default, there is absolutely no audio recorded when you record your display screen. If you wish to record your tone of voice narrating along when you record the display, for example, all you need to do will be to change one particular setting.

ON your iPhone, swipe down at the upper-right corner of the screen.

Tip: *You can certainly do this from your lock screen or even whilst your iPhone 12 is unlocked.*

1. **Press** and **hold the Screen Record** symbol.

2. Tap **Mic On**.

3. Tap **Start recording**.

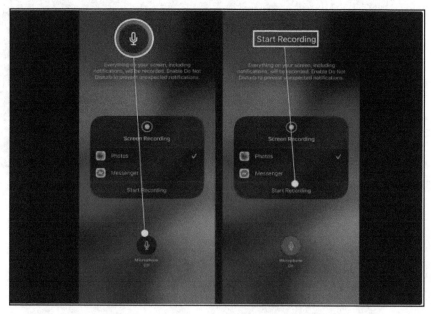

4. You're now saving your display screen with sound to interact with it.

5. To stop recording your screen, tap the **red status**

bar at the very top left hand side of the screen.

6. Tap **Stop**.

7. The video is automatically saved to **Gallery**.

How to Adjust Screen Recording Settings

Briefly, you can't. The only real option is, the possibility to adjust will be the capability to take up a Facebook Messenger broadcast rather than recording and saving for your Photos. It isn't possible to regulate the resolution as well as the video's high quality from the clip.

Once the display Recording is saved, you'll be able to *trim and edit* the online video via the Photos app's capabilities.

Limitations For Recording Your Screen

You can't record everything on your iPhone 12. The issue here is that you can't record loading apps like **Netflix**, **Disney** or **Amazon**, **Prime Movie**. That's because normally it might be feasible to pirate the displays you're streaming which may be contrary to the conditions and terms of using the service.

Generally, though, it is possible to record anything on your iPhone 12 including clips of games you're taking part in.

Tip: *Notifications and calls* may also be recorded so you might wish to change the ***Do Not Disturb*** *settings* once you make a display recording.

Chapter 3

iPhone 12 and AirPods

The *iPhone 12* does not come with *AirPods*. The *iPhone 12* doesn't include any headphones or perhaps a power adapter. It just includes a *USB cable. Apple* says it eliminated the earphones and power adapter to lessen packaging and weight of materials.

Do AirPods come with iPhone 12?

With the launch of the iPhone 12, lots of people are preparing to upgrade. And if you are upgrading your cell phone, it is also a good period to upgrade some other key add-ons like your headsets. That leads lots of people to inquire: *"Do AirPods comes with iPhone 12?"*

It is a pretty organic question. In the end, the iPhone and AirPods make a fantastic combo and when you're spending $100s (or thousands in some instances) of dollar as the case may be on a brand-new phone, it seems sensible that you may get additional cellular headphones included.

Nicely, we're sorry to inform you: Air-pods aren't incorporated with the **iPhone 12**. *No matter what choice of the iPhone you're buying, any from the iPhone 12 model, or any previous model, you need to buy Air-pods individually.*

We recommend **Air-pods** especially the *sound-canceling Air-pods*, Pro-thanks to their excellent audio quality and awesome features, but you will need to budget a supplementary couple of hundred bucks to get them.

The iPhone 12's Missing Headphones

To make issues worse, Apple has introduced a noticeable change to what components it offers with brand-new iPhones. Before, a brand-new iPhone was included with a charging cable, an electrical adapter to plug into walls stores, and wired earphones (lately Apple's Air-pods). Any longer.

You start with the iPhone 12, you merely get the charging wire. *The iPhone no more includes the power adapter or, most of all, the Air-pods headsets.*

That is right: you start with the iPhone 12, you do not get any earphones with your iPhone.

Apple states this move was created to reduce product packaging, and thus waste materials and shipping excess weight. The company will be touting this within its dedication to the surroundings.

In a few ways, this is practical. It's true that will reduce the environmentally friendly footprint from the iPhone 12. Furthermore, most people currently have headsets of some sort, so the incorporated Air-pods will be duplicative, and possibly wasteful.

Alternatively, this does look like an effort by Apple to drive people towards purchasing expensive **Air-pods**. As mentioned earlier, Air-pods are great and worth the purchase price, but it doesn't make sure they are any cheaper.

Tip: As the iPhone 12 might not include Air-pods, it can provide a ton of great benefits. We've divided all of the most important information regarding the iPhone 12.

Headphone Choices for iPhone 12

Since *Air-pods* isn't added in the *iPhone 12*, and neither carry out any other earphones, what are your alternatives? Practically anything!

It is possible to still buy *Air-pods* from Apple for approximately **$19**. And you may buy the second-generation Air-pods for about **$160** or the **Air-pods Pro** for about **$250**.

But you may also get just any other sort of headsets, too. The iPhone facilitates almost any Bluetooth earphones, including Apple's type of Beats headsets.

If you like wired headphones apart from the Air-Pods, ensure you get the $9 adapter to plug the typical headphone jack port into Apple's Lightning slot at the bottom of the iPhone *(the iPhone 12 doesn't use USB-C. Probably the iPhone 13 will?)*.

How to Shut down iPhone 12

What to Know

- **Press** and **hold** the **Side button** and possibly

Volume Up or even **Volume Down** before the slider appears near the top of the **Screen**.

- Then move the Slide to **power off** the slider completely to the end.
- To turn the **iPhone 12** back **ON**, press and hold the side button before the Apple logo design appears on the screen.

This short description explains how exactly to power the *iPhone 12* and turn it *ON* again. Besides, it addresses any conditions that could appear when attempting to switch off the smartphone.

Besides a minimal battery, you may even want to shut down the *iPhone 12* in case your iPhone will be acting strange. Rebooting an *iPhone* will be a good solution to solve all sorts of issues. Whatever your cause, you can switch off the iPhone 12 by pursuing these actions:

1. *Press and hold the side button* and possibly **Volume Up** or **Volume Down** for seconds. Once the slider appears near the top of the display, release the buttons.

Tip: On older models, holding down the medial side

button was enough, however, now that activates **Siri**.

2. Move the **Slide** to the right to shut down the phone.

3. A progress bar will appear at the heart of the display screen. A couple of seconds later, the iPhone becomes off.

Tip: Want to switch off your iPhone 12 to save lots of battery life? It isn't your only choice. If you wish to preserve battery while nevertheless having the ability to make use of your iPhone, attempt **Low Power Setting**. We likewise have other ideas to save iPhone battery existence.

How to Power Off iPhone 12 when the Basics won't Work

In some instances, your iPhone may be malfunctioning in a manner that prevent it from turning off most commonly. If you adhere to the methods above and your *iPhone 12* won't turn off, you might need to get one of these different techniques.

If so, you need to use what's known as a *'force restart'* or perhaps a *'hard reset.'* This can be a kind of restart that clears all the iPhone's active memory space (don't worry;

you will not lose any information like pictures and communications) and is most beneficially used when it will not respond to regular means of switching off the iPhone 12.

How To Start The iPhone 12

If you've successfully turned off your *iPhone 12*, eventually you will have to learn how to start the iPhone 12 again. To achieve that, press and hold the *Side button*. Once the *Apple logo* appears on the screen, release the side switch. The phone will boot up in a couple of seconds.

How to Restart iPhone 12

Once in a while, you'll probably have to restart the **iPhone 12**. It is possible to restart an iPhone to resolve problems like *bad Wi-Fi connection, app crash, or other mini bugs*. Whether you will need a regular restart or perhaps a hard reset which depends on your situation.

- The typical restart turns the **iPhone Off** and turns it **On** again. That is also known as a ***Normal*** *restart*.

If the typical restart doesn't repair your issue or the iPhone is frozen and unresponsive, a force restart (also be called a *hard reset*) could work.

To restart an iPhone 12, follow these actions:

1. **Press** and **hold** the *Side button* and *Volume down button*.

Tip: The *Volume Up button* works, too, but if you are using that and do not time it very correctly, you might accidentally have a *screenshot*.

2. After a couple of seconds, the slide to turn off the phone will appear on the screen. At that time, *release the Side* and *Volume Down buttons*.

3. *Move* the slider to shut down the phone.

Tip: *Been considering cleansing your iPhone display?* Doing it when the cell phone is turned off. That way, you will not accidentally push anything within the display screen or mistakenly switch your settings.

4. Wait around *15-30 seconds* for that iPhone to carefully *turn Off*. Once the iPhone is off and it's been 15-30 seconds, *press down the side* button

again before the *Apple logo* shows. Release the Side button and allow *iPhone 12* restart.

How to Force Restart iPhone 12

The typical restart can fix plenty of numerous problems, nonetheless, it won't fix all of them. In case your iPhone 12 is frozen and pushing the side button doesn't perform anything-you have to try to force restart iPhone 12. Here's how:

- Press the *Volume Up* key once.
- Press the *Volume Down* key once.
- **Press** and **hold** the *Side button*. **Hold** until you start to see the Apple logo. Disregard the slide to power off the slider when it turns up. When the Apple logo appears, release the Side key.
- Wait while your iPhone 12 restarts.

Chapter 4

iPhone 12 and iPhone 12 Pro Guidelines

Simply get yourself an *iPhone 12* or an *iPhone 12 Pro*? You've obtained the fastest smartphone on earth, and that as well by a very long shot. It includes Apple's most recent *A14 Bionic chipset, uses 5G connection,* and sports an unbelievable *Super Retina XDR screen,* among plenty of some other new features. If you just found your *iPhone 12* or *iPhone 12 Pro,* listed below are a number of guidelines that you need to remember while you go about making use of it.

1. Move from iPhone

If you're to upgrade from a previous iPhone, don't forget to move your data firstly. That way, you can avoid needing to set up your *iPhone 12 or iPhone 12 Pro* from scrape.

While you can perform that over **iCloud**, a faster way would be to transfer your computer data directly from your previous iPhone (If you still have it accessible).

After turning On your *iPhone 12*, stick it close to your old iPhone and connect both phones to power. You need to see the *Fast boot* screen on your old *iPhone*. Adhere to the *onscreen guidelines* and select *Exchange from iPhone* to exchange your data rapidly.

2. Understand 5G Icons

After many years of hype and gossips, you get 5G connectivity on the iPhone 12. This allows for amazing download and upload rates of speed as high as *4.0 Gbps and 200 Mbps*, respectively. With this comes three various status icons that you might want to look out for - *5G, 5G+, and 5GUW.*

5G - Indicated regular 5G network availability.

5G+/5GUW - Indicated faster high-frequency 5G network availability.

3. Manage Smart Data Mode

5G is amazing. Nonetheless, it may also ding your iPhone's battery strength. To create that much less of a concern, your *iPhone 12* or *iPhone 12 Pro* features *Smart*

Information Mode, a feature that switches between **5G** and **4G** based on network activity.

For instance, you won't want *5G* while scrolling down your Twitter and Facebook timelines. Wise *Data Mode* can make your iPhone make use of *4G* in those situations. But if you opt to download a movie on *Apple TV*, your *iPhone 12 Pro* automatically takes the benefit of a faster *5G*.

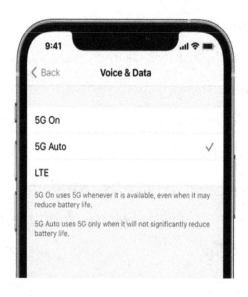

It is possible to manage *Smart Information Setting* via *Settings > Cellular > Voice & Information*. Select **5G** to enable *Wise Data Setting* or **5G** to disable the features - the second option setting will force your iPhone to Use *5G* regularly but may find yourself draining your electric battery.

4. Restrict 5G

Smart Data Setting aside, you can even limit your iPhone 12 or even *iPhone 12 Pro* from making use of 5G (except during movie loading) by switching on **Low Power Mode**. *Go to Settings > Electric battery to carefully turn it ON.* On the other hand, you can Tap the ***Low Power Mode icon*** in the ***Control Center*** to carefully turn it **ON**.

5. Don't Just Forget about Magsafe

Your brand-new *iPhone* includes a ***MagSafe connector***. It includes a range of magnets in the back that allows you to snap on a bunch of *add-ons* from cellular chargers, wallets, to wise cases. Browse the ***MagSafe Add-on*** section on the *Apple Store* for plenty of cool items that you should use.

6. Purchase 20w USB-C Power Adapter

Your *iPhone 12* might not feature a charging adapter, nonetheless, it sure includes a Power to *USB-C* wire for quick charging. Therefore, consider grabbing an electrical adapter having a ranking of *20W* or more rather than sticking with your aged *5-10W* charger.

7. 5G iOS Updates

Because of 5G connectivity, it is possible to download *OTA* (*over-the-air*) **iOS** updates using mobile data. To ensure that it's possible, head to *Configurations* > *Cellular* > *Information Mode* and choose to *Allow More* Information on **5G**.

8. FaceTime HD Calls

For the first time with an iPhone, it is possible to do **Face**

Time video calls in *1080p HD*. Head to *Configurations > Cellular > Information Mode* and choose to Allow More Information on **5G** to **Face Time** in HD over 5G. You can even do this by linking to **Wi-Fi**.

9. Take better Low-Light Photos

Don't be timid to shoot pictures with your **iPhone 12** and **iPhone 12 Pro** in low-light situations. The bigger *f/1.6 aperture* within the Wide camera can catch 27% more lighting, allowing for pictures that appear incredibly better in comparison to similar photos for the *iPhone 11 lineup*.

10. Take and Edit 10-little bit HDR Video

The **iPhone 12** can shoot a 10-bit Dolby Eyesight HDR movie at 30fps, as the **iPhone 12 Pro** ramps that to 60fps. You can even edit captured video clips on your iPhone itself via the typical Photos app.

11. AirPlay 4K HDR Content

When you have a second-gen **Apple TV** or an **AirPlay**

2-enabled intelligent TV, it is possible to **AirPlay 4K HDR** content making use of your **iPhone 12** or **iPhone 12 Pro.**

12. Quick Take Videos

Quick Take can be acquired on additional **iPhones**. But it's a remarkably useful feature which should come in very handy once you want to take a quick movie. Instead of fumbling around changing to Video setting on your **iPhone 12** or **iPhone 12 Pro**, tap and contain the Shutter symbol to start documenting video with Fast Consideration. Swipe your hand to the right if you wish to switch to movie recording completely.

13. Take Advantage of LiDAR

The triple-lens camera array on the **iPhone 12 Pro** includes a **LiDAR (Light Recognition and Ranging) sensor**. It Uses lasers to a step's distance, which brings about plenty of benefits. For instance, your brand-new iPhone can offer superior Augmented Fact experiences, therefore don't forget to hop to the **App Store** to test some **AR Apps**. To create things better still, LiDAR also enhances auto-focusing by around six times, assisting you to capture better photos and movies.

14. Snap Portraits in Night Mode

Both **iPhone 12** as well as the **iPhone 12 Pro** supports **Night mode** on leading and the back cameras. But over the **iPhone 12 Pro**, in particular, you can even capture Night Setting portraits with the back camera. That's made possible because of the enhanced auto-focusing as a result of the **LiDAR sensor**.

15. Shoot in Apple ProRAW

Your **iPhone 12 Pro** includes a fantastic triple *12MP camera* array comprising a broad, an ultra-wide, along with a phone lens. It permits amazingly detail-rich pictures, especially using the Apple A14 Bionic's sophisticated computational photography functions at play.

Having said that, your **iPhone 12 Pro** also supports a brand-new imaging format called **Apple ProRAW**. As its title implies, it is possible to shoot pictures and videos within the Green format minus the elegant camera effects, letting you have the ultimate say by editing and enhancing them however you want.

Apple ProRAW won't be accessible If you just got your **iPhone 12 Pro** on the launch date. Rather, the Cupertino-based technology giant is meant to include it in another **iOS update**.

16. Customize Home Screen

With **iOS 14**, it is possible to completely customize the home screen on your **iPhone 12** or **iPhone 12 Pro** with the addition of and modifying *Home display widgets, removing unwanted apps, hiding whole Home screen pages, etc.*

17. Watch Video clips in Picture-in-Picture Mode

iOS 14 lets you watch videos inside the Picture-in-Picture setting. Swipe up while you're watching a movie in a full-screen setting, and you ought to see the movie show up inside a floating PiP pane instantly. The functionality functions on apps such as example *Apple TV, Hulu, and Netflix*. You can even watch YouTube in a Picture-in-Picture setting.

18. Watch YouTube in 4K

Talking about YouTube, **iOS 14** brings assistance for **Google's VP9 codec**. This means you can watch YouTube in every of its 4K on your iPhone 12's spectacular Super Retina XDR screen. While you're watching a backed video clip on YouTube, talk about the Quality choice menu and choose 2160p to change to 4K.

19. Face Time Eye Contact

It is possible to complement **Face Time HD** on the **iPhone 12** and **iPhone 12 Pro** with **Eye Contact**. As soon as enabled, the function can make it appear just like you are looking straight at the individual on another end instead of in the camera. To make it possible, head to *Configurations > Face Time and start the switch close to Eye Contact.*

20. Change Default Browser

With **iOS 14**, you don't need to be stuck using browser or the default Mail app. Rather, you can set up any other backed third-party browser or e-mail client (such as Chrome) to operate because of the default.

To achieve that, dive into the Settings app on your **iPhone 12** or **iPhone 12 Pro** and choose the app that you would like to help make the default. After that, tap Default *Internet browser App/Default Email App* and designate the app because of the default.

21. Manage Your Privacy

When you are using the best smartphone on the market, you must furthermore keep an eye on your privacy. Fortunately, **iOS 14** includes plenty of privacy-related configurations and options that will help you need to do that.

Chapter 5

The iPhone 12 Cameras & Voice Mail

Key Takeaways

- Even the tiniest *iPhone 12 mini* has much better cameras than very last year's *iPhone 11 Pro*.

- The *iPhone 12 Pro Max* gets almost all cool camera features.

- Low-light and nighttime pictures get way much better.

Aside 5G and MagSafe. The reason to get this year's iPhone will be its digital camera. Or, digital cameras, plural. They're simply amazing.

Even the tiniest, cheapest *iPhone 12 mini* gets (nearly) all of the functions from last year's Pro models, as well as the **iPhone 12 Pro**, displays what can be performed once you connect ultra-powerful computers with cameras. But regrettably, it's still only a *"cell phone,"* meaning many *pro photographers* will never actually consider it.

A Quick Look at the Numbers

Let us have a look at some of the most essential new features of the **iPhone 12** and **iPhone 12 Pro**:

- All iPhones now captures **Night Mode**, catch video in **Dolby Eyesight HDR**, and make use of **Deep Fusion**.
- All iPhones possess *optical picture stabilization*.
- *The iPhone 12, as well as the iPhone 12 mini both, have a similar camera.*
- Both **iPhones Pro (Normal and Max)** put in a telephoto camera, **Apple ProRAW**, and Nighttime Portraits.
- The *iPhone Pro Max* includes a bigger sensor on the primary (wide) camera, a far more powerful

telephoto zoom lens, and techniques the sensor rather than the zoom lens for better image stabilization.

It's an elaborate lineup, however now you might have the gist of the various functions which are usually distributed in number. Now, let's drill down in.

Night Life

Last maiden edition, the iPhone 11, the iPhone cameras took a revolution, rivaling standalone cameras, and surpassing them in lots of ways.

Among the neatest methods was **Night Setting**, which uses picture processing to fully capture incredibly fine detail at night scenes, while even now looking like these were taken during the night (Google's edition can make night time shots appear to be daytime). That's available nowadays in all digital cameras on the iPhone, not only the wide digital camera.

However, the Pro requires things more; the *LiDAR digital camera* that Apple devotes to the **iPad Pro** is now within the **iPhone 12 Pro**. LiDAR builds a 3D level map of the scene (it's used by self-driving vehicles to instantly chart their environment), also it works at night. The 12 Pro uses this chart to get nearly instant autofocus at night, also to enable the background-blurring, family portrait mode on Night mode pictures. It's an incredible trick.

The 12 Pro Max also gets a larger sensor on its main (wide) camera. Larger sensors mean larger pixels, this means even more light could be gathered.

ProRAW

Before you watch it, an iPhone photo has undergone trillions of digesting operations, because of the onboard supercomputer. Several images are usually merged, the backdrop will be blurred, and the info from your sensor will be interpreted to produce a picture. On the iPhone 12 Pro, many of these steps are stored alongside the picture in Apple's brand-new **ProRAW** format.

You know ways to edit an image within the Photos app, then return anytime to tweak it? It is possible to, for example, put in an awesome B&W filtration system and change the backdrop blur, then half a year later, it is possible to get back to adjust the blur without influencing the rest of one's edits.

ProRAW offers the same degree of modular tweaking, just with all of this deep-level running. It also helps you to save the *"green"* data result through the sensor. You can do it yourself within the Pictures app, however, the *ProRAW format* may also be opened up to designers. You'll have the ability to edit in **Lightroom**.

How to Setup Voicemail on iPhone 12

What to Know

- For any generic greeting head to *Cell phone > Voicemail > Setup Now > develop a password > Default > Save.*

- To record the custom message head to *Phone > Voicemail > Create Now > develop a security password > Select Custom Made > Record > Stop.*

- For both choices, tap **Play** to hear the greeting, and tap **Save** if you are content with the recording.

This steps above walks you through the procedure of

establishing your voicemail on iPhone 12, demonstrates how to access visual voicemail, and strategies for managing your voicemail box.

Among the initial things, you will most probably wish to accomplish when you get the iPhone 12 would be to get the voicemail set up.

The good information is that when you've set up voicemail on an iPhone before, that is still the same procedure. If you're not used to the iPhone, nevertheless, an instant tutorial is available below.

1. To begin with, go directly to the *Mobile phone app* on your **iPhone 12**.

2. Touch the **Voicemail icon**. This appears like two circles, linked by a right line at the bottom.

3. If it's the very first time you're accessing voicemail, you will see an option to create your voicemail. Touch *Set Up Right Now*, to begin with the creation process.

4. When prompted, develop a voicemail security password. The security password should be 4-6 digits long.

Tip: Select a password that you will be able to keep in mind. If you forget your password, there is no solution to reset it from your iPhone. Instead, you will have to get in touch with your service provider to request of them to reset it.

5. Then you will be prompted to select or develop a greeting. It is possible to select Default or Custom.

- **Default:** The default greeting that prompts the caller to keep a message.

- **Custom:** It is possible to custom record with the info you want to include.

If you choose Custom **Tap Record** to begin with saving your greeting. If you are *done*, tap **Quit**. If you wish to evaluate the voicemail, tap **Play** to hear the greeting you're recorded.

6. When you're content with your voicemail information, tap **Save** to perform the voicemail set up process.

How does Your Carrier affect Your Voicemail Settings?

Before, some mobile service carriers had different instructions for establishing voicemail, just how you set the service up depends on the carrier which offered your mobile service. Contemporary cellphones have built-in voicemail applications, therefore establishing voicemail is fairly consistent across service providers.

Is iPhone Voicemail like Visual Voicemail?

You might see voicemail on your iPhone 12 known as *Visual Voicemail*. Visible Voicemail will be voicemail having a visual interface, just like a voicemail app. It lets you see and choose your voicemail communications, so you need not pay attention to them within the order these were received. It is possible to, instead, pay attention to your voice mails within the order you like, skipping around, and also not hearing messages, if you like.

Visual Voicemail can be acquired on almost all mobile service provider networks, so it is apt to be the default voicemail for the iPhone 12.

Note: If you wish to double-check if Visual Voicemail can be acquired from your provider, Apple maintains a summary of providers that assist with the feature.

How to Setup Visual Voicemail Transcription on iPhone 12

Like Visual Voicemail, most US companies also assist with voicemail transcription, which is on iPhone 12. To access a transcript of the voicemail on your device adhere to these guidelines:

1. Start by opening the *phone app* on your **iPhone 12**.
2. Tap **Voicemail**.
3. The first time you tap any recent voicemail, the app will start transcribing the message. Following a couple of seconds, the transcription should be seen within the voicemail page.

If you see blank lines within the transcription *(__)*, those are missing terms that we're unable to be transcribed because of the information being garbled or unclear.

4. After the transcription is complete, it is possible to touch the **Share button** to deliver the voicemail transcription via **AirDrop, Mail, or iMessage**.

Managing Your iPhone 12 Voicemail

There will come a period you'll want to switch your

voicemail password or greeting. Or possibly you dislike the default voicemail notification audio and desire to change it. All are simple options to regulate.

- **To improve your voicemail greeting:** Head to *Cell phone > Voicemail and tap Greeting.* Then stick to the prompts to improve the greeting.

- **To improve your voicemail security password:** *Head to Settings > phone > Switch Voicemail Password and enter the brand new password you intend to use.*

- **To improve voicemail notification sounds:** *Head to Settings > Sounds & Haptics > New Voicemail then choose the sound you intend to use from your Alert options.*

- **To make a call from the voicemail:** Tap a voicemail to open up it and tap the decision Back option.

- **To delete a voicemail:** Touch a voicemail to open it up and tap **Delete**. Remember that some providers may instantly delete a voicemail totally, so whether it's something you imagine you might like to get back, you ought not to delete it.

Chapter 6

How to Customize iPhone

Customize iPhone Home Screen

You may take a look at your *iPhone home screen* more than some other single screen so that it should be set up the way you want it to appear. Below are a few options for customizing your iPhone *home screen*.

- *Change Your Wallpaper*: You may make the image behind your applications on the home screen just about whatever you want. A favourite picture of your children or spouse or the logo design of your preferred team is a few options. Find the wallpaper settings by heading to *Settings -> Wallpaper -> Select a New Wallpaper*.

- *Use Live or Video Wallpaper*: Want something eye-catching? Use cartoon wallpapers instead. There are a few restrictions, but this is relatively cool. *Head to Settings -> Wallpaper -> Select a New Wallpaper -> pick and choose Active or Live.*

- *Put Apps into Folders*: Organize your home screen centred on how you Utilize applications by grouping them into folders. Begin by gently tapping and securing one application until all your apps begin to tremble. Then pull and drop one application onto another to place those two applications into a folder.

- *Add Extra Webpages of Apps*: All your apps won't need to be about the same home screen. You may make individual "webpages" for different kinds of applications or different users by tapping and keeping applications or folders, then dragging them from the right side of the screen. Browse the *"Creating Web pages on iPhone"* portion of How to Manage Apps on the iPhone Home Screen to get more.

Customize iPhone Ringtones & Text Message Tones

The ringtones and text tones your iPhone uses to get your attention need not be exactly like everyone else's. You may make all types of changes, including changing the sound, and that means you know who's phoning or texting without even taking a glance at your phone.

- **Change the Default Ringtone**: Your iPhone comes pre-loaded with a large number of ringtones. Change the default ringtone for all those calls to the main one you prefer the better to get notified when you experience a call to arrive. Do this by *heading to Settings -> Noises (Noises & Haptics on some models) -> Ringtone.*

- **Set Person Ringtones**: You can assign a different ringtone for everybody in your connections list. That way, a love track can play whenever your partner calls, and you know it's them before even looking. Do that by heading to *Phone -> Connections -> tapping the individual whose ringtone you want to improve -> Edit -> Ringtone.*

- **Get Full-Screen Photos for Incoming Phone calls**: The incoming call screen does not have to be boring. With this suggestion, you can view a fullscreen picture of the individual calling you. Go to *Mobile phone -> Connections -> touch the individual -> Edit -> Add Picture.*

- *Customize Text Tone*: Like everyone else can customize the ringtones that play for calls, you can customize the appearance like video when you get texts. Go to *Configurations -> Seems (Noises & Haptics on some models) -> Text message Tone.*

TIPS: *You're not limited by the band and text tone that include the iPhone. You can purchase ringtones from Apple, and some applications help you create your tone.*

Customize iPhone Lock Screen

Like everyone else, you can customize your home screen; you can customize the iPhone lock screen, too. In this manner, you have control over the very first thing you see each time you wake up your phone.

- *Customize Lock Screen Wallpaper*: Exactly like on the home screen, you can transform your iPhone lock screen wallpaper to employ a picture, computer animation, or video. Browse the link within the last section for details.

- *Create a Stronger Passcode*: The much longer your passcode, the harder it is to break right into your iPhone (you are utilizing a passcode, right?). The default passcode is 4 or 6 character types (depending on your iOS version); nevertheless, you make it much longer and stronger. *Head to Settings -> Face ID (or Touch ID) & Passcode -> Change Passcode and following an instructions.*

- *Get Suggestions from Siri*: Siri can learn your practices, preferences, passions, and location and then use that information to suggest content for you. Control what Siri suggests by heading to *Configurations -> Siri & Search -> Siri Recommendations and setting the things you want to use to On/green.*

iPhone Customizations that makes things Better to See

It isn't always a simple text message or onscreen items on your iPhone, but these customizations make things much simpler to see.

- *Use Screen Focus*: Do all the onscreen symbols and text message look a little too small for your eye? Screen Move magnifies your iPhone screen automatically. To Utilize this option, go to *Settings -> Screen & Brightness -> View -> Zoomed -> Collection.*

- *Change Font Size*: The default font size on your iPhone may be a little small for your eye; nevertheless, you can raise it to make reading convenient. Head to *Settings -> General -> Availability -> Larger Text message -> move the slider to On/green -> change the slider below.*

- *Use Dark mode*: If the shiny colours of the iPhone screen strain your eye, you may choose to use

Dark Setting, which inverts shiny colours to darker ones. Find the essential Dark settings in *Configurations -> General -> Convenience -> Screen Accommodations -> Invert Colours.*

Customize iPhone Notifications

Your iPhone helpfully notifies you to understand when you have calls, text messages, emails, and other bits of information that may interest you. But those notifications can be irritating. Customize how you get notifications with these pointers.

- *Choose Your Notification Style*: The iPhone enables you to choose lots of notification styles, from simple pop-ups to a mixture of sound and text messages, and more. Find the notification options in *Settings -> Notifications -> touch the application you want to regulate -> choose Alerts, Banner Style, Noises, and more.*

- *Group Notifications from the Same App*: Get yourself many notifications from an individual app, but won't need to see each one taking space on your screen? You can group notifications into a *"stack"* that occupies the same space as your notification. Control this on the per-app basis by heading to *Settings -> Notifications -> the application you want to regulate -> Notification Grouping.*

- ***Adobe flashes a Light for Notifications***: Unless you want to try out to get a notification, you may make the camera adobe flashlight instead. It's a delicate, but apparent, option for most situations. Set this up in *Settings -> General -> Convenience -> Hearing -> move the LED Screen for Notifications slider to On/green.*

- ***Get Notification Previews with Face ID***: In case your iPhone has Face ID, you can utilize it to keep the notifications private. This establishing shows a simple headline in notifications; however, when you go through the screen and get identified by Face ID, the notification expands, showing more content. Establish this by going to *Settings -> Notifications -> Show Previews -> When*

Unlocked.

TIPS: That link also offers an excellent tips about using Face ID to silent alarms, and notification sounds, i.e., *"Reduce Alarm Volume and Keep Screen Shiny with Attention Awareness."*

Get more information with Notification Centre Widgets: *Notification Centre* not only gathers all your notifications, but it also offers up widgets, mini-versions of applications to enable you to do things without starting apps whatsoever.

Other iPhone Customization Options

Here's an assortment of a few other different ways to customize your iPhones.

- ***Delete Pre-Installed Apps***: Got a couple of applications pre-installed on your iPhone you don't use? You can delete them (well, the majority of them, anyhow)! Just use the typical way to delete apps: Touch and keep until they tremble, then tap the x on the application icon.

- **Customize Control Centre**: *Control Centre* has a lot more options that are apparent initially. Customize Control Centre to get just the group of tools you want to use. Head to *Settings -> Control Centre -> Customize Settings.*

- **Install your preferred Keyboard**: The iPhone includes an excellent onscreen keypad; nevertheless, you can install third-party keyboards that add cool features, like *Google search, emojis, and GIFs, plus much more.* Get yourself a new keyboard at the App Store, then go to *Settings -> General -> Keyboard -> Keyboards.*

- **Make Siri a friend**: Choose to have Siri talk with you utilizing a man's tone of voice? It could happen. Head to *Settings -> Siri & Search -> Siri Tone of voice -> Male.* You can even go with different accents if you want.

- **Change Browser's default search engine**: Have search engines apart from Google that you'd like to use? Make it the default for those queries in Browser. Head to *Settings -> Browser -> Search*

Engine and making a new selection.

- *Make Your Shortcuts*: If you an iPhone 11 or newer version user, you can create all sorts of cool customized gestures and shortcuts for various jobs.

- *Jailbreak Your Phone*: To get the most control over customizing your mobile phone, you can jailbreak it; this gets rid of Apple's settings over certain types of customization. Jailbreaking can cause functional problems and lessen your phone's security, but it can give more control.

Chapter 7

Siri on iPhone 12

How to Make Use of Siri on iPhone 12

What to Know

- *You can find two methods to access Siri on iPhone 12 models:* long-pressing the right-side button or having a voice command, like *"Hey Siri."*

- Siri no more takes over all of your screens, instead of functioning with a colorful symbol and widget reactions.

- You should use Siri to announce messages to other Apple products like *Home Pods* and *Air Pods* via *an intercom-like mode.*

This information below explains how exactly to enable and access Siri on the iPhone 12, your skill using the voice assistant, and how to use the intercom feature.

How to Enable Siri on iPhone 12

Before you make use of the brand-new features which were released on Siri in iOS 14, you need to make sure that Siri is allowed on your iPhone 12.

1. Open **Settings**.

2. Select **Siri & Search**.

3. Then on the Siri & search page, make certain the next three choices are allowed:

- *Listen to "Hey Siri":* Allowing you to state the wake term *"Hey Siri"* to begin with an interaction using the voice assistant.

- *Press the Side button for Siri:* This enables you to wake Siri by long-pressing the button on the right side of the mobile phone.

- *Allow Siri When Locked:* Allowing you to use Siri without unlocking your phone.

How to Make use of Siri on iPhone 12

As soon as Siri is enabled on your *iPhone 12*, to access it, all you have to accomplish is either state *"Hey Siri"* or even long-press the key on the right side of the mobile phone.

Using the Siri update in iOS 14, the voice assistant no more gets control of your full screen. Rather, you will see a vibrant icon at the bottom of the display to point that Siri will be hearing your query or request. After that, when responding, the replies can look like widgets and banners on some of your cell phone screen, however, they still won't take over the complete display.

Improvements to Siri in iOS 14

The *iOS 14 update to Siri* (that is the version installed on iPhone 12 during release) included several updates towards the voice assistant's appearance and abilities. Beyond the looks changes which were mentioned previously, these features had been also additional or enhanced:

- *Better Answer:* Siri manages more than 25 billion demands per month, by *Apple*. To discipline all those demands, the *VA* has had to understand a lot. Apple promises that *Siri* offers 20 times even more facts than it does a couple of years ago. As well as the digital assistant's capability to use the internet to provide solutions has also been enhanced.

- *Smarter Suggestions:* On the list of enhancements to Siri is a useful widget for *Shortcut Suggestions* which allows **Siri** to suggest activities that you carry out regularly. For instance, when you enter the automobile, Siri might recommend starting *maps*, or *purchasing a coffee from your favorite coffee home*. And, you could have these suggestions on your home display screen.

- *ETA sharing:* If you are conferencing another iPhone consumer and you wish to provide them with an ETA, it is possible to ask Siri to *"Talk about my ETA."* Siri will deliver your ETA, via *Apple Maps*, compared to that individual. There are always a handful of caveats, though. You 'must' have already started instructions in Apple Maps, as well as your **Apple ID** email will undoubtedly be used to talk about your estimated introduction time.

- *Voice Messaging:* Siri may record and send sound messages for you using **iMessage** or even **MMS texts** (therefore you may also send audio recordings to Android customers). Just state *"Send an audio information to"* and **Siri** will record and deliver the audio. You should have the option to hear it, cancel it, or rerecord it before you decide to send the information. You'll also have the choice to get this done through *Car Play*.

- *Better Translation:* The translation solutions that have been obtainable through Siri have improved with iOS 14. Nowadays there are *65 language sets* and you won't need to get linked to the web for that translation to occur. Also, the translations are usually very much better than they were.

- *Cycling Directions With Maps*: If you want cycling directions, now you can inquire Siri, *"What exactly are cycling directions to [title of destination or location]."* If Siri doesn't realize or recognize the area you've requested instructions for, the tone of voice assistant will offer you suggestions, and redirect you to Apple Maps for the correct directions.

- *Automated Reminders From Email:* In iOS 14, Siri acquired the capability to identify feasible reminders from e-mail and create suggestions. If you discover you develop a large number of reminders from the e-mail, this is a useful function to help keep you on your game.

How to Make use of Siri as an Intercom

One additional function that you might find helpful when working with Siri for the iPhone 12 may be the intercom function that can be found if you have multiple Apple gadgets in your home. The intercom function can be acquired across Apple-wise home products, such as **iPhones, iPads, Apple Watch, Air Pods, and also CarPlay.**

To use the function say, *"Hey Siri, say to everyone [your information]."* Siri will deliver the communications to connected gadgets, and recipients can react by stating, *"Hey Siri, replay [their reaction].*

Messages which are sent via the intercom function will be fun-filled on *HomePod products and AirPods* and can appear as notifications on gadgets such as **iPhone and iPad.**

Chapter 8

How to Take Screenshot on iPhone 12

What to Know

- Press **Volume Up** and the side button at the same time to capture the *screenshot*.

- *Screenshots* are usually saved for your Pictures app, within the Screenshots section.

- To share the screenshot, open up the Pictures app, tap the *screenshot* > *Talk about* > *select app*.

This section explains how to have a screenshot on *iPhone 12*, where to find them, and how to share them.

Going for a screenshot on the iPhone 12 is a superb way to store a meaningful information, an excellent joke, or another important moment. While you can find third-party apps that get screenshots, it's not necessary. The capability to have a screenshot within the iPhone 12 is made into iOS. Some tips about what you must do:

1. Get anything you would like as screenshot on your iPhone. This may be a text, a page, or something within an app.

2. Press the side button and the volume up button at

the same time.

3. Once the screen flashes and you also hear a camera sound, which means you took a screenshot. The thumbnail from the screenshot seems within the lower-left corner.

4. To save the screenshot and not do anything else with it, swipe it from the edge of the screen. If you wish to edit or interact with the screenshot, touch the thumbnail.

How to Find Your iPhone 12 Screenshot

Once you have a screenshot about *iPhone 12*, the screenshot is saved to a particular folder within your phone's pre-installed Pictures app. To see a screenshot, adhere to these actions:

1. Tap the **Pictures app**.

2. If **Albums** isn't currently selected at the underneath bar, **tap it**.

3. **Scroll down** and **tap Screenshots**. This is a collection of every screenshot you have taken.

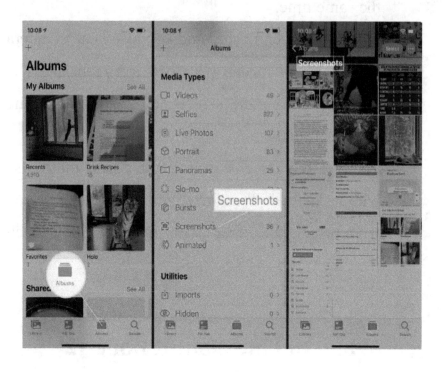

4. Your screenshots may also be inside your Camera album, mixed along with some other photos.

How to Share iPhone 12 Screenshots

Once you have got the screenshot saved on your iPhone 12, it is possible to share it the same method you would any picture: via *textual content, email, on social media, etc*. You can even delete it or sync it to your personal computer. Follow these methods to share a screenshot:

1. In the Pictures app, find and locate the screenshot

within the *Camera Album* or the *Screenshots Album*. After that tap the *screenshot* to open it up.

2. Tap the **Share button**.

3. Tap the app you intend to use to share the screenshot.

4. If you tapped an app in the next row it'll open. Complete sharing using the ways that are particularly compared to that app.

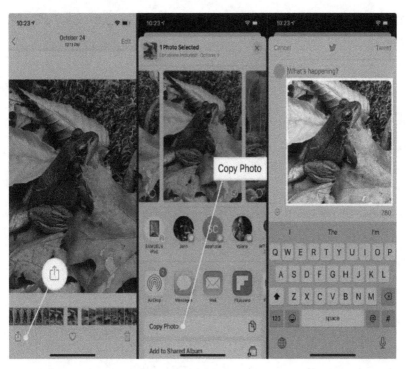

How to Close Apps on iPhone 12

What to Know

- Swipe right up from underneath of the display,

swipe left to get the app you intend to close up, then wipe it right up and off the top of the display screen.

- It is possible to quit several apps at the same time by swiping them at the same time using several more fingers.

- There is absolutely no built-in solution to clear all apps simultaneously.

This information below explains how to close apps within the iPhone 12. Also, it dispels the misunderstanding that giving up apps to save lots of battery life.

Closing apps may also be called *stopping apps, force stop apps, or force closing apps.*

To close apps on the iPhone 12, follow these steps:

1. From any screen on the iPhone 12 (the home screen or in an app), swipe up from underneath the screen. It is possible to swipe so far as you need, but about 25% up will do.

2. This reveals all the apps which are running on your iPhone 12.

3. Swipe backward and forwards to see every one of the apps.

4. When you discover the one you intend to quit, swipe it upward and off the top of the screen. If they disappear from your display, the app will be closed.

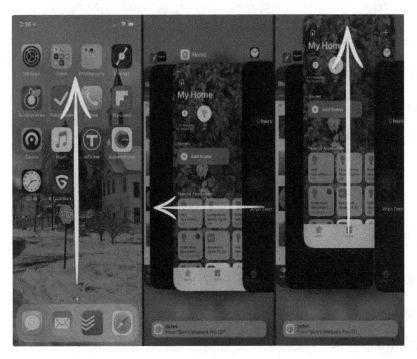

Tip: *It is possible to quit several apps at the same time. Simply swipe all of them at once making use of several more fingers.*

5. Three is the Max number of apps you could close at the same time on the iPhone 12. There is absolutely no built-in solution to obvious close all apps simultaneously.

When You Should Close iPhone Apps

When you're not using an iPhone app, it switches into the background and it is frozen. This means that this app uses fairly little battery existence and likely will not make use of any data. Generally in most cases, a freezing app is equivalent to one which has been shut. The major distinction that a frozen app restart quicker than an app that's shut when you release it.

Close Apps That Are Not Working

As a result of this, the only time you will need to close up or even quit iPhone apps is when the app isn't functioning. If so, stopping and restarting the app could solve a short-term bug, just as restarting your iPhone can.

Some apps may ask the machine to alow it a particular number of time and power to finish an activity or even to continue operating because that is the whole reason for the app (think songs, mapping, and marketing communications apps).

Chapter 9

iTunes, iCloud & Android Backup

Restore

There is no need connecting your brand-new iPhone to your personal computer, as long as there is a mobile data connection designed for activation. As you end the set-up wizard, you may navigate back by tapping the back arrow at the top left-hand side of the screen and scroll further to another display by tapping another button at the top right-hand corner.

You can commence by pressing down the power button

at the top edge of your brand-new iPhone. You may want to keep it pressed down for about two seconds until you notice a vibration, meaning the iPhone is booting up.

Once it boots up finally, you can start initial set up by following the processes below;

- Swipe your finger over the display screen to start the *set-up wizard*.
- Choose the *language of preference* - **English** is usually at the top of the list, so there is no problem finding it. However, if you would like to apply a different language, scroll down to look for your desired **language**, and tap to select the preferred language.
- Choose your **Country** - the *United States,* for instance, which may be close to the top of the list. If otherwise, scroll down the list and select the *United States* or any of your choice.
- You need to connect your iPhone to the internet to start its activation. You can test this via a link with a *Wi-Fi network*. Locate the name of your available network in the list shown, and then tap on it to select it.

- Enter the *Wi-Fi security password* (you will generally find this written on your router, which is probably known as the *WPA Key, WEP Key*, or *Password*) and select **Sign up**. A tick indication shows you are connected, and a radio image appears near the top of the screen. The iPhone would now start activation with Apple automatically. It may take some time!

- In case your *iPhone* is a *5G or 4G* version, you would be requested to check for updated internet configurations after inserting a new *Sim card*. You can test this anytime, so, for the present time, tap **Continue**.

- *Location services* would help you with *mapping, weather applications*, and more, giving you specific information centred wholly on what your location is. Select whether to use location service by tapping allow location services.

- You would now be requested to create **Touch ID,** which is Apple's fingerprint identification. **Touch ID** allows you to unlock your iPhone with your fingerprint instead of your passcode or security password. To set up *Touch ID*, put a finger or your thumb on the home button (but do not press it down!). To by-pass this for the moment, tap **setup Touch ID** later.

- If you are establishing *Touch ID*, the tutorial instruction on the screen will walk you through the set-up process. Put your finger on the home button, then remove it till the iPhone has properly scanned your fingerprint. Whenever your print is wholly scanned, you would notice a screen letting you know that tap recognition is successful. Tap **Continue**.

- You would be requested to enter a passcode to secure your iPhone. If you create **Touch ID**, you must use a passcode if, in any case, your fingerprint isn't acknowledged. Securing your computer data is an excellent idea, and the iPhone provides you with several options. Tap *password option* to choose your lock method.

- You can prepare a *Custom Alphanumeric Code* (that is a security password that uses characters and figures), a *Custom Numeric Code* (digit mainly useful, however, you can add as many numbers as you want!) or a *4-Digit Numeric Code.* In case you didn't install or set up **Touch ID,** you may even have an option not to add a Security password. Tap on your selected Security option.

- I would recommend establishing a 4-digit numeric code, or *Touch ID* for security reasons, but all optional setup is done likewise. Input your selected Security password using the keyboard.

- Verify your Security password by inputting it again. If the Password does not match, you'll be requested to repeat! If indeed they do match, you'll continue to another display automatically.

At this time of the set-up process, you'll be asked whether you have used an iPhone before and probably upgrading it, you can restore all of your applications and information from an *iCloud or iTunes backup* by deciding on the best option. If this is your first iPhone, you would have to get it started as new, yet, in case you are moving from Android to an iPhone, you can transfer all your data by deciding and choosing the choice you want.

How to Restore iPhone Back-up from iCloud or iTunes

If you want to restore your iPhone from an iTunes back-up, you may want to connect to iCloud and have the latest version of iTunes installed on it. If you are ready to begin this process, tap **restore** from iTunes back-up on your iPhone and connect it to your personal computer. Instructions about how to bring back your data can be followed on the laptop screen.

In case your old *iPhone model* was supported on *iCloud*, then follow the instructions below to restore your applications & data to your brand-new device:

- Tap *Restore* from *iCloud back-up.*

- Register with the **Apple ID** and Password that you applied to your old iPhone. If you fail to recollect the security password, there's a link that may help you reset it.

- The ***Terms & Conditions*** screen would show. Tap the links to learn about specific areas in detail. When you are ready to proceed, select **Agree**.

- Your iPhone would need some moments to create your **Apple ID** and hook up with the *iCloud server.*

- You would notice a summary of available backups to download. The most up-to-date backup would be observed at the very top, with almost every other option below it. If you want to restore from a desirable backup, tap the screen for ***all backups*** to see the available choices.

- Tap on the back-up you want to restore to start installing.

- A progress bar would be shown, providing you with a demo of the advancement of the download. When the restore is completed, the device will restart.

- You would see a notification telling you that your iPhone is updated effectively. Tap *Continue*.

- To complete the iCloud set up on your recently restored iPhone, you should re-enter your **iCloud** (*Apple ID*) password. Enter/review it and then tap *Next*.

- You'll be prompted to upgrade the security information related to your *Apple ID*. Tap on any stage to replace your computer data, or even to bypass this option. If you aren't ready to do this, then tap the *Next* button.

- **Apple pay** is Apple's secure payment system that stores encrypted credit or debit card data on your device and making use of your iPhone also with your fingerprint to make safe transactions online and with other apps. Select *Next* to continue.

- To *feature/add a card*, place it on a set surface and place the iPhone over it, so the card is put in the camera framework. The credit card info would be scanned automatically, and you would be requested to verify that the details on display correspond with your card. You'll also be asked to enter the *CVV* (safety code) from the personal strip behind the card. If you choose (or the camera cannot recognize your cards), you can enter credit card information by hand by tapping the hyperlink. You could bypass establishing **Apple Pay** by tapping *create later*.

- Another screen discusses the *iCloud keychain*, which is Apple's secure approach to sharing your preserved security password and payment information throughout all your Apple devices. You might use *iCloud security code* to validate your brand-new device and import present data, or you might be asked to continue registering your keychain if it's your first Apple device. In case you don't want to share vital data with other devices, you should go to *avoid iCloud keychain* or *don't restore passwords*.

- If you selected to set up your *Apple keychain*, you'd be notified to either uses a Security password (the same one you'd set up on your iPhone or provide a different code. If you're making use of your iCloud security code, you should put it on your iPhone when prompted.

- This would confirm your **ID** when signing on to an iCloud safety code; a confirmation code would be delivered via *SMS*. You may want to hyperlink your smartphone text code (if you have never distributed one with Apple already) so that the code may be provided as a text. Then enter this code to your iPhone if requested, then select *Next.*

- You'll then be asked to create **Siri**. *Siri* is your own digital personal associate, which might search the internet, send communications, and check out data in your device and a lot more, all without having to flick via specific apps. Choose to create *Siri* by tapping the choice or start *Siri* later to skip this task for now.

- To set up and create *Siri,* you would need to speak several phrases to the iPhone to review your conversation patterns and identify your voice.

- Once you say every term, a tick would be observed, showing that it's been known and comprehended. Another phrase may indicate that you should read aloud.

- Once you've completed the five phrases, you

would notice a display notifying that Siri has been set up correctly. Tap *Continue*.

- The iPhone display alters the colour balance to help make the screen show up naturally under distinctive light conditions. You can switch this off on the screen settings after the iPhone has completed configuring it. Tap *continue* to continue with the setup.

- Has your iPhone been restored? Tap begin to transfer your computer data to your brand-new iPhone.

- You'll be prompted to ensure your brand-new iPhone has enough power to avoid the device turning off in the process of downloading applications and information. Tap *OK* to verify this recommendation.

- You would notice a notification show up on your apps to download in the background

How to Move Data From an Android Phone

Apple has made it quite easy to move your data from a Google Android device to your new iPhone.

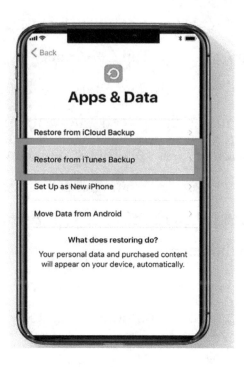

Proceed to the iOS app. I'll direct you on how to use the application to move your data!

- Using the iPhone, if you are on the applications & data screen of the set-up wizard, Tap *move data from Google Android*.

- Go to the Play Store on your *Google Android* device and download the app recommended by the set-up wizard. When it is installed, open up the app, select **Continue,** and you'll be shown the *Terms & Conditions* to *continue*.

- On your Android device, tap *Next* to start linking your Devices. On your own iPhone, select

Continue.

- Your iPhone would show a 6-digit code that has to be received into the **Google Android** device to set the two phones up.

- Your Google android device would screen all the data that'll be moved. By default, all options are ticked - so if there could be something you don't want to move, tap the related collection to deselect it. If you are prepared to continue, tap *Next* on your Google android device.

- As the change progresses, you would notice the iPhone display screen changes, showing you the position of the info transfer and progress report.

- When the transfer is completed, you will notice a confirmation screen on each device. On your Android Device, select *Done* to shut the app. On your iPhone, tap *Continue*.

- An *Apple ID* allows you to download apps, supported by your iPhone and synchronize data through multiple devices, which makes it an essential account you should have on your iPhone! If you have been using an older model of iPhone previously, or use iTunes to download music on your laptop, then you should have already become an **Apple ID** user. Register with your username and passwords (when you have lost or forgotten your **Apple ID** *or password*, you will see a link that may help you reset it). If you're not used to iPhone, select doesn't have an **Apple ID** to create one for *Free*.

- The Terms & Conditions for your iPhone can be seen. Please go through them (tapping on more to study additional info), so when you are done, tap *Agree*.

- You'll be asked about synchronizing your data with iCloud. That's to ensure bookmarks, connections, and other items of data are supported securely with your other iPhone's data. Tap *merge* to permit this or ***don't merge*** if you'll have a choice to keep your details elsewhere asides *iCloud*.

- **Apple pay** is Apple's secure payment system that stores encrypted credit or debit card data on your device and making use of your *iPhone* also with your fingerprint to make safe transactions online and with other apps. Select *Next* to continue.

- To *feature/add a card*, place it on a set surface and place the iPhone over it, so the card is put in the camera framework. The credit card info would be scanned automatically, and you would be requested to verify that the details on display correspond with your card. You'll also be asked to enter the *CVV* (safety code) from the personal strip behind the card. If you choose (or the camera cannot recognize your cards), you can enter credit card information by hand by tapping the hyperlink. You could bypass establishing **Apple Pay** by tapping *create later*.

- Another screen discusses the *iCloud keychain*, which is Apple's secure approach to sharing your preserved security password and payment information throughout all your Apple devices. You might use *iCloud security code* to validate your brand-new device and import present data, or you might be asked to continue registering your keychain if it's your first Apple device. In case you don't want to share vital data with other devices, you should go to *avoid iCloud keychain* or *don't restore passwords*.

- If you want to set up your *Apple keychain*, you'd be notified to either use a Security password (the same one you'd set up on your iPhone or produce a different code. If you're making use of your *iCloud* security code, you should put it on your iPhone when prompted.

- This would confirm your **ID** when signing on to an iCloud safety code; a confirmation code would be delivered via SMS. You may want to hyperlink your smartphone text code (if you have never distributed one with Apple already) so that the code may be provided as a text. Then enter this code to your iPhone if requested, then select *Next.*

- You'll then be asked to create **Siri**. *Siri* is your own digital personal associate, which might search the internet, send communications, and check out data in your device and a lot more, all without having to flick via specific apps. Choose to create *Siri* by tapping the choice or start **Siri** later to skip this task for now.

- To set up and create *Siri*, you would need to speak

several phrases to the iPhone to review your conversation patterns and identify your voice.

- Once you say every term, a tick would be observed, showing that it's been known and comprehended. Another phrase may indicate that you should read aloud.

- Once you've completed the five phrases, you would notice a display notifying that Siri has been set up correctly. Tap *Continue*.

- The iPhone display alters the colour balance to help make the screen show up naturally under distinctive light conditions. You can switch this off in the screen settings after the iPhone has completed configuring it. Tap *continue* to continue with the setup.

- Has your iPhone been restored? Tap begin to transfer your computer data to your brand-new iPhone.

- You'll be prompted to ensure your brand-new iPhone has enough power to avoid the device turning off in the process of downloading applications and information. Tap *OK* to verify this recommendation.

- You would notice a notification show up on your apps to download in the background.

NB: Setting up any new iPhone model: A similar method, as described above, applies.

Chapter 10

How to Restart an iPhone

The iPhone is a robust computer that ties in a pocket. As being a pc or laptop, sometimes an *iPhone* must be restarted or reset to repair a problem. To restart an iPhone, turn it Off, then turn it On. When an iPhone doesn't respond to a restart, execute a reset. Neither process deletes the info or configurations on the iPhone. These aren't exactly like a restore, which erases all this content on the iPhone and returning it to manufacturing conditions, and you restore your computer data from a back-up.

How to Restart the New iPhone

Restart an iPhone to resolve fundamental problems, such as poor *mobile or Wi-Fi* connectivity, application crashes, or other day-to-day glitches. On these models, Apple designated new functions to the *Sleep/Wake button* privately for these devices. It could be used to activate *Siri*, talk about the Emergency SOS feature, or other tasks. As a result of this change, the restart process differs from the technique used in previous models.

To restart an iPhone 12, iPhone 11, iPhone X, and iPhone 8:

- Press and hold the *Sleep/Wake* and *Volume Down* buttons at the same time. *Volume up* works, too, but utilizing it can unintentionally create a screenshot.

- When the slide to power off slider shows up, release the Sleep/Wake and Volume Down buttons.

- Move the slider from left to shut down the phone.

How to Restart Other iPhone Models

Restarting other iPhone models is equivalent to turning the iPhone On/Off. Beow are some tips on what to do:

- ***Press and contain the Sleep/Wake button***: On old models, it's at the top of the phone. On the iPhone 6 series and newer, it's on the right hand side of the phone.

- When the power off slider appears on the screen,

release the *Sleep/Wake* button.

- *Move the power off slider from left to right*: This gesture prompts the iPhone to turn off. A spinner shows on the screen indicating the shutdown is happening. It might be dim and hard to see.

- When the phone turns off, press and hold the *Sleep/Wake button.*

- When the *Apple logo* appears on the screen, release the *Sleep/Wake button*, and await the iPhone to complete restarting.

How to Hard Reset an iPhone

The essential restart solves many problems, but it generally does not answer all of them. In a few cases, such as when the phone is completely freezing and won't react to pressing the Sleep/Wake button, a better option called a **hard reset** is necessary.

On *iPhone 12, iPhone 11, iPhone X, and iPhone 8 series*, the hard reset process differs from other models. To hard reset these iPhone models:

- Click and release the *Volume Up* button.

- Click and release the *Volume down* button.

- Press and hold the *Sleep/Wake button* before gliding to power off slider appears.

- Move the slip to force off slider from left to reset the phone.

How to Hard Reset Other iPhone Models

A hard reset restarts the phone and renewes the memory space that applications run in. It generally does not delete data but usually helps the iPhone begin from scratch. Typically, a hard reset is not needed, however when it is necessary on a mature model (except iPhone 7), follow these steps:

- With the phone screen facing you, press down the *Sleep/Wake* button and the home button at the same time.

- Continue to hold the control keys when the power

off slider shows up, don't release the control keys.

- When the *Apple logo* appears, release the *Sleep/Wake button* and the *home button*.

- Wait as the iPhone resets.

How to Hard Reset iPhone 7 Series

The hard reset process is somewhat different for the *iPhone 7 series*. That's because the home button is not a physical button on these models; it's a **3D Touch -panel**. Because of this, Apple transformed how these models are reset.

Using the iPhone 7 series, keep the *Volume Down button* pressed, and the *Sleep/Wake button* at the same time.

More Help Resetting Your iPhone

Sometimes an iPhone may have problems so complicated a restart or reset doesn't work. Follow these advanced troubleshooting steps to fix the problem:

- *Stuck at Apple Logo*: If an iPhone is stuck at the *Apple logo* during startup, a straightforward restart might not be adequate to solve the problem. I recommend taking the iPhone to a professional or *Apple repair centre*.

- ***Restore to Manufacturing default Settings***: If you wish to erase all the info from an iPhone and begin from inception, this solves some hard bugs. Before you sell your iPhone, restore it to *factory settings*.

- ***Recovery Setting***: If an iPhone is stuck at a reboot loop or can't get past the Apple logo during startup, try *iPhone recovery mode*.

- ***DFU Mode***: When downgrading the version of the *iOS* or jailbreak the phone, use *DFU (Disk Firmware Update) mode*.

Chapter 11

How to Show Battery Percentage on an iPhone 12

What to Know

- Swipe straight down from the top right corner of the display. The battery portion is at the top right corner close to the battery symbol.

- **Tap** and **hold** the screen before icons begin wiggling. *Touch + > Batteries > pick the widget design > Include Widget > Done.*

The information below explains how to watch the battery percentage on the iPhone 12 in addition to how to have it on your home screen using a widget.

On previous versions of **iOS**, you'd like to turn **ON** the battery percentage substitute for seeing these details. Not over the *iPhone 12*! Nowadays, the electric battery percentage option will be on by default you have to understand where to locate it.

Tip: If you're upgrading from an iPhone without **Face ID**, you will see that due to the camera notch at the very top, there is no plenty of room to show the electric battery icon as well as the percentage simultaneously.

1. Swipe lower from the top right corner of the *iPhone 12 display screen* to open *Control Center*.

2. At the top right corner of the screen, close to the battery icon, the battery percentage. This is one-way the electric battery your iPhone 12 have left.

3. Swipe up or even tap the background to close ***Control Center***.

If all you have to accomplish is periodically check out the battery strength, then that's all you need to do. If you wish to easily track the battery's standing, consider including a widget on your home screen.

Tip: One method to find the electric battery percentage for iPhone 12 would be to ask Siri. **Activate Siri.** Using the Side button and inquire *"Hey Siri, just how much battery do I have remaining?"* The electric battery percentage may appear on the screen.

How to add Battery Widget to an iPhone 12

Because of widgets in iOS 14, which shows up pre-loaded within the iPhone 12, you can include a battery percent widget on your home display. Here's how:

1. **Tap** and *hold the screen* before icons begin *wiggling*.
2. Tap +.
3. In the widgets pop-up, tap *Batteries*.
4. Pick the widget design you intend to make use of. Swipe backward and forward to start to see the choices. The Batteries widget may also show battery pack info for Apple devices linked to your cell phone like *Apple Watch or AirPods*.

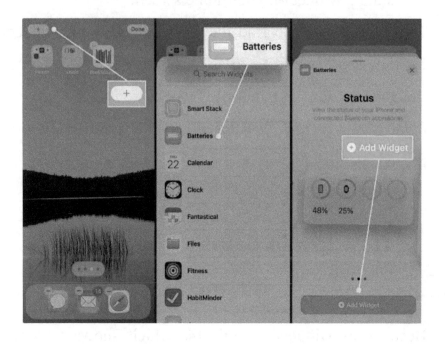

5. Tap *Add Widget* for the main one you intend to use.

6. The widget is add on your home screen. Proceed it on to the positioning where you need it and tap **Done**.

How to Make use of Apple Pay on iPhone 12

What to Know

- Double-press the switch on the right side of the mobile phone, authorize with your **Face ID** and hold your cell phone near the transaction terminal.

- In Apple Budget, tap + to include a new transaction card; cards linked to your Apple accounts may already be listed.

The information discussed in this section includes instructions on how best to set up **Apple Pay** with an **iPhone 12** and how exactly to use it to create payments at **NFC terminals**.

Apple Pay is a handy function of current iPhones, and undoubtedly it's on iPhone 12. If you have never used it before, here is a fast guide to setting it up to set up.

1. To find **Apple Pay,** tap *Resources > Wallet.*

2. A conclusion of how Apple Pay functions appear on the display. Read it and tap **Continue**.

3. Tap **Credit** or **Debit Card** to choose an existing card or put in a new card.

4. If you can find cards linked with your *Apple account*, they'll appear on another screen. If one particular is the credit card you intend to use, ***choose it.***

5. To add a brand-new card, tap **Add a Different Card**.

Tip: *When you have zero cards mounted on your account, you might only have the choice to add a brand-new card.*

6. You will be prompted to scan a card. Do this, and then Tap **Continue**.

Tip: *If the card won't check out, you can even enter the card information manually.*

7. You will be promoted to include the protection code for that card. Do this and tap **Continue**.

8. Once the cards continue to be added, you'll get a confirmation screen. Tap **Continue**.

Note: You might be prompted to learn and consent to the Conditions and Terms. If so, go through the offered information and Tap **Agree**. If you tap **Disagree** you will not have the ability to add your transaction card.

9. Another explanation screen appears which outlines how to use **Apple Pay**. Go through it and Tap **Continue** to go back to your **Wallet**.

How to Make use of Apple Pay in-store

Once you have added a minimum of one card to your **Apple Wallet**, you can use Apple Payout in participating shops to create contactless obligations. This only functions to get accepted by **Apple Pay**.

Once you see one particular symbol that follows these instructions:

1. Double-press the medial side key on the right side of the iPhone 12.

2. **Apple Pay** starts for your default card. Keep your mobile phone up and authenticate the deal using **Face ID**.

Note: You can even work with a different credit card when you have several within your wallet. As soon as your default card appears, touch it and choose the credit card you intend to use.

3. Then hold the phone close to the payment terminal and soon you would see **Done** along with a blue checkmark displayed on your screen.

How to Change Your Default Card on Apple Pay on iPhone 12

If you just have one card in Apple Payout, it becomes your default transaction credit card. When you include other credit cards or change credit cards, you might like to set another card in place of the default.

The simplest way to perform it is to open the **Wallet**, and *tap and hold the card you intend to make your default.* After that, drag that credit card to the leading of all cards you might have listed. This can ensure it is the default.

If you're having difficulty with this technique, here's an alternative solution to help make a different card the default:

1. Open up the **Settings app**.
2. Scroll straight down and tap **Finances & Apple Pay**.
3. Tap **Default Credit card**.
4. Select the *new credit card* you intend to use as a default.

Next time you double-press the *side button* to initiate **Apple Pay**, the card you selected as the new default would be the card that will appear.

Chapter 12

iOS 14

Apple in June 2020 introduced the most recent version of the *iOS operating system, iOS 14*, that was released on Sept 16. iOS 14 will be among Apple's latest iOS updates up to now, introducing *Home display design changes, main new features, up-dates for present apps, Siri enhancements, and many some other tweaks that streamline the iOS user interface.*

First of all, iOS 14 brings a redesigned *Display Screen* which includes assistance for widgets for the very first time. Widgets could be dragged from your watch onto the home screen, and maybe pinned in various sizes.

With a good Stack function, the iPhone may use on-device intelligence to surface the right widget predicated on time, location, and activity. Each *Home Screen* page can show widgets personalized for *work, journey, sports, and much more*. The area where widgets are usually homed also has already been redesigned, and there is a widgets gallery where customers can pick brand-new widgets from apps and customize those widgets.

Swiping completely to the end from the app pages on an iPhone starts the brand new App Library, which is an interface that presents all the apps on your iPhone to find out everything instantly. Apps are structured into the folder program, but there's also Apple-created folders like *Recommendations* and *Apple Arcade* that intelligently surface area apps. New app downloads could be added to your *Home Screen* or held within the *App Library* to help keep your *Home Display* cleaner.

New space-saving steps mean incoming calls and *Siri* requests no more take over the complete screen. Calls (*and Face Time/VoIP phone calls*) arrive in a little banner on the iPhone's screen while activating *Siri* displays a mini cartoon Siri icon at the bottom of the display screen.

With an image in *Picture mode*, users can observe videos or talk on *FaceTime* while also using other apps at the same time, with *FaceTime* or perhaps a video playing in a little window that may be resized and relocated to any corner from the *iPhone's screen*.

Siri is smarter on iOS 14 and will answer a larger range of queries with information pulled from over the web, and Siri may also send sound messages. Keypad dictation operates on a device, including an additional coating of personal privacy for dictated messages.

Apple added ***App clips*** to *iOS 14*, making users benefit from some app functions without having to download the entire app. App Videos can enable you to do things such as rent a mobility scooter, purchase an espresso, make a cafe reservation, or fill up a car parking meter simply by checking a code, without the necessity to download a complete app.

Apple describes App clips as only a *"mini section of a good app Face"* made to be within the moment it is needed. *App Videos sort out Apple-designed App Clip rules, NFC tags, or QR rules, and can furthermore be discussed in Communications or from Browser.*

Talking about the *Text messages app*, Apple now lets customers pin a significant conversation such that it remains near the top of the app. Communications could be pinned with a straightforward swipe to the right on any. A brand-new inline replies function may be used to reply to a particular message in a conversation, which is especially helpful in team chats.

For group discussions, Apple added an *@mention* function, which means an organization chat could be muted but sends a notification whenever a user's title is mentioned. Team chat photos could be customized by having a picture or an emoji, as well as the icons for every person near the top of a discussion, inform you who was final speaking.

Brand-new **Emoji** *options are offering additional hairstyles, headwear, face coverings, and ages, plus brand-new emoji stickers for a hug, fist bump, and blush.* **Emoji** tend to be more expressive than ever because of the revamped cosmetic and muscle framework.

Combined with watchOS 7, iOS 14 allows parents to set up and manage mobile **Apple Watches** for his or her babies through **Family Setup**, made to allow kids to make use of an Apple Watch with no need to have an iPhone.

For medical apps, Apple has added support for *Sleep Tracking on Apple Watch*, and also a *Health Checklist for managing safe practices functions* **(Emergency SOS, Medical ID, Fall Detection, and ECG)** *and addition to greatly help users better know how audio amounts make a difference hearing health.*

In the weather app, there is information on severe weather events, a next-hour precipitation chart, and minute-by-minute precipitation readings when the weather is forecast, all functions adopted from Apple's *Dark Sky acquisition.*

The Apple Maps app has bicycling directions for bicycle commuters and cyclists, using the directions considering elevation, how busy a road is, and whether you can find stairs along the way. For individuals with personal electric automobiles, there's a choice to the path with **EV** getting stops personalized for current automobile and charger sorts.

A curated Guide shows list of interesting locations to

visit in a town for finding brand-new dining places and attractions. Manuals are manufactured by trusted manufacturers just like the Washington Article, All Trails, Complex, Periods Group, and much more.

Digital car secrets let customers unlock or start their vehicle having an *iPhone* or *Apple Watch*, and then a year, using the **U1 chip**, the automobile keys let customers unlock vehicles without getting the iPhone from a wallet or bag. Vehicle keys could be shared through Text messages and handicapped via **iCloud** if an iPhone is lost.

CarPlay lets customers set wallpapers also helps new app varieties for parking, electric powered automobile charging, and fast food ordering.

The Home app is smarter with automation suggestions and Handle Center fast access buttons, plus an Adaptive Illumination feature lets Home Kit lights adjust their color temperature during the day.

On-device Face Recognition lets digital cameras and movie doorbells tell customers exactly who reaches the entranceway (predicated on Individuals saved in

Pictures), and Home Kit Safe Video cameras assistance Activity Areas for the very first time

There is a new *Apple-designed* **Translate app** that delivers textual content and voice translations to and from 11 dialects. An On-Device Setting lets languages become downloaded for on-device translations just, along with a Discussion Mode talks translations aloud, therefore, users can talk to someone that talks a different vocabulary, and it instantly detects the vocabulary becoming spoken and translates rightly

Supported languages consist of *Arabic, Chinese, British, French, German, Italian, Japanese, Korean, Portuguese, Russian, and Spanish.*

Up-to-date privacy protections need developers to obtain permission before being able to access devices on an area network, and you can find new choices for restricting access to choose photos or offering apps with just approximate location data. All apps may also be required to obtain user authorization before monitoring them across web sites, and new symbols arrive on the home Display screen when an app will be using a digital camera or microphone.

What Does iOS 14 Protection Features Mean to You And Your iPhone?

Privacy is a big section of Apple's technique for building the iPhone uniqueness towards the variety of Android products you must pick from. The *iOS 14* update has a sponsor of new functions that only additionally boost Apple's lead in the area.

iOS 14, available these days in a public beta, is touting several privacy-led features that are likely to assist you to have a far more secure smartphone Face than before.

These are made to be used by the average individual, and these aren't simply necessarily for individuals who come in a type of function where they have to consider their privacy.

But are these functions likely to impact how you use your phone? Just time will tell, but we've explored a number of the important features arriving at your iPhone - and can likely be prepared and waiting on the iPhone 12 - that could ensure it is safer to use than ever.

Transparency is a big deal

Much like any technological system, your iPhone apps are usually tracking you while you navigate around your iPhone. Understanding what these apps are usually tracking will be what's essential, and iOS 14 was created to make it simpler than ever to understand what information you're sharing.

Apple is getting significant changes to the App Store to be sure all apps have an inventory that lets you know just what this app may monitor. For instance, when the app says your location and may read your contact number, you'll find out that before you've downloaded it on your device.

Apple is making certain all developers need to include that info within the app list itself. In case a program doesn't consist of that details, the app will not be allowed in the App Store.

Independent cybersecurity analyst *Graham Cluley* told TechRadar, "Anything which raises transparency in regards to what apps are usually doing must be good information for consumer privacy, therefore I welcome this task.

"If the typical consumer will focus on authorization notifications such as other issue entirely. Everybody knows that many of us just click through any authorization screens without reading through (or at the very least knowing) the implications of what they will have just decided to."

It'll be as much as the user to choose whether they'll Use this info, but even though you don't do that some other iOS 14 functions already are improving components of other apps.

iOS 14 beta includes a banner to verify once you paste from another gadget (eg copy on the Mac PC and paste on iPhone) Appears to be bugging away.

Since this personal privacy issue was discovered, TikTok has promised to avoid the app from achieving this potential and which should make it a lot more secure for several users instead of those who find themselves actively concerned about their privacy.

Does this mean there will be fewer apps?

Not every organization will necessarily get the same precautions mainly because of TikTok, and there's usually the opportunity we'll see fewer third-party apps for the store because of this.

Having said that, it's likely Apple will undoubtedly be good with losing that little minority of designers who don't follow these guidelines. Cluley feels that almost all developers will adhere to these guidelines, as well.

He said, "I'd suppose any app which tried to sneak through outrageous levels of monitoring and data selection without being open and transparent on any of it with Apple and customers would end up potentially facing analysis from App Store.

"It wouldn't help to make business feeling to upset individuals who work your only path to iPhone clients."

Location improvements

Another security-led feature within iOS 14 is that you

will be able to talk about your "approximate location" having an app instead of your exact location. Just what this implies - such as distance or period when your area is documented - is usually unclear at this time.

Cluley said, "Most apps that require your location don't need your precise area. This can be a very sensible stage for people's privacy and personal security."

There may be quite a few apps that you would like to talk about your exact location with. For instance, you might want **Apple Maps** or **City mapper** with an accurate reading on where you are usually, but *do social media apps need to find out more than the town you're in?* Now you can decide that within iOS 14.

What does this all mean?

As Cluley notes, the features iOS 14 units out is only going to be as good as they seem if individuals begin to use them. There's no assurance these features will undoubtedly be harnessed by the average individual, but also for anyone seeking to be more safety-conscious, this can help.

Another brand-new feature is your phone's status bar will light having an indicator if an app is obstructing the use of your microphone or camera. That'll be useful to those that understand what it means, but unless you realize it, you're unlikely to know whether it's a concern or not.

On the main topics of whether iOS may be the preferred system, Cluley says this individual believes many personal privacy-conscious individuals will choose Apple's operating-system already.

He said, "Android phones are working an operating-system run by way of a huge marketing company, which earnings from what they can find out about their customers. Apple has differentiated themselves in their approach.

"Needless to say, OS choice isn't the only area of the equation. Third-party apps and solutions introduce privacy dangers and conditions that are usually platform

impartial - although it's good if ora can boost a caution)."
These improvements might not switch everything on
your iPhone, but iOS 14's minor movements ensure it is
that tiny bit better and make the use of your iPhone a
little bit safer.

Complete Five Actions On Start or Setup Wireless Carplay on iPhone

Step 1. *Go to the Configurations app on your iPhone Home Display.*

Step 2. *Navigate to General.*

Step 3. *You will need to tap CarPlay.*

Step 4. Right now if Bluetooth will be turned off on your iPhone, after that you'll get yourself a pop-up.

Tap on ***Start Bluetooth***. if bluetooth won't function then ***Repair BT*** on your handest from the soft restart.

Step 5. *Press and holdn the Tone of a voice control button on your Steering bar to start **CarPlay Setup**.*

Now after setting up wireless **CarPlay** on iPhone. Enjoy all feasible iPhone functions throughout your car driving.

Troubleshooting

- iPhone 5 or even Later Siri should be turn on, Go directly to the *Settings > Siri & Research appear between your Wallpaper and Face ID/Touch ID/ Security password tabs > change toggle On/Green for Listen to "Hey Siri", Push side button for* **Siri** *and invite Siri when locked.*

- Check, your vehicle Stereo helping *AirPlay*.

- Your *Carplay* is supporting Wireless or **USB**,

check it out on **CarPlay** slot marked with Smartphone icon or *CarPlay icon*.

- The car is running motion, make certain about that

- Quick hardware problems: Restart *iPhone*, Switch *USB cable*, Update to the most recent *iOS version*, Also the firmware is usually updated in a stereo system.

Chapter 13

iPhone 12 Cheat Sheet

What are the essential features of the iPhone 12 model?

5G Network:

The 5G technologies in every four brand-new iPhone 12 versions facilitate both *sub-6GHz and Wave systems*. The sub-6GHz range is even more pervasive, can go farther, and it is even more resistant to disturbance. But it is also even more crowded, restricting its actual velocity. On the other hand, Wave is a lot faster but is definitely even more susceptible to disturbance and so is most effective only at a closer range to cellular towers. In America, *AT&T, T-Mobile, and Verizon* Cellular offer both forms of systems, but Wave is the up-and-comer, specifically by *Verizon*.

The main carriers have already been rolling out their 5G networks, but access, especially in America, remains limited by major cities. Therefore, unless you reside in the right place you're not likely to observe better overall performance with only a 5G smartphone.

Adding 5G will help make the iPhone 12 lineup more future-proof, like 5G ought to be more ubiquitous in a year or two as protection expands. This element is essential since budget-conscious individuals are keeping their smartphones more time than previously. Needless to say, *Samsung* along with other *Google Android phone vendors* have already been equipping their cell phones with *5G*, therefore *Apple* requires the feature only if to stay competing.

Since *5G* could be a drain in the electric battery, Apple has wisely introduced a good *Data Mode function*. When 5G isn't needed, the phone instantly drills right down to 4G.

Processor:

The most recent iPhones are driven by the brand new A14 Bionic processor chip, which is furthermore within the **2020 iPad Air 4** introduced in Sept. As Apple's innovative mobile chip, however, the A14 was created to enhance performance and save well on electric battery life. The brand new *six-core processor chip* offers four high-efficiency cores and two high-performance cores.

Using a new and innovative *5nm* course of action, this latest chip house *11.8 billion transistors*, up through the

8.5 billion in continue year's *A13 Bionic. The bigger transistor count implies that the A14 isn't just quicker but even more power-efficient.* Shifting from 8 to 16 cores, the *A14's* neural motor can perform 11 trillion cycle per second, growing the rate of computations and device learning.

Display:

All new iPhones have active **OLED** screens fitted with Apple's Super Retina XDR screen and High **Definition Range (HDR)**. Supplying a 2,000,000:1 comparison percentage and 1,200 nits of optimum brightness, they are a few of the most sophisticated screens ever included in an iPhone. Used together, these functions provide superior picture quality, more power efficiency, more precise colors, and much better contrast over traditional LCD screens.

Ceramic Shield Screen:

Through a function known as *Ceramic Shield*, the iPhone 12 consists of ceramic in its front side cup display, thus producing the display tougher and much more fall resistant. This technique works by including a brand-new high-temperature crystallization technique that develops nano-ceramic crystals in the cup matrix. Predicated on Apple's screening, *Ceramic Shield* escalates the iPhone 12's fall efficiency by four occasions on the iPhone 11.

Rear Digital Cameras:

The **iPhone mini** and **iPhone 12** have two *12-megapixel back cameras*--one wide and ultra wide. The **iPhone 12 Pro** and **iPhone 12 Pro Max** possesses three 12-megapixel back cameras--*wide, ultra wide, and telephoto*. Plus, both Pro models use the fourth zoom lens for **LiDAR mapping** to gauge the range and level of objects even more accurately, an attribute of great benefit to augmented fact apps. The broad camera offers an *f/1.6 aperture*, the fastest yet with an iPhone, which Apple says provides 27% more lighting in low-light disorders.

The *12-megapixel telephoto cameras* within both **iPhone 12 Pro** choices offer an *f/2.0 aperture* having a *52mm focal length, a 4x or 5x optical focus variety, and optical picture stabilization.*

On the movie front, the back cameras of the iPhone 12

mini and iPhone 12 can take HDR movie with Dolby Vision around *30 fps*, as the ones on both Pro iPhone 12 versions can capture HDR movie with Dolby Vision around *60 fps*.

Front camera:

The iPhone 12's front-facing 12-megapixel digital camera provides an *f/2.2 aperture* and will shoot *HDR movie* with Dolby Eyesight around *30 fps*.

Quick Take:

Introduced with iOS 13 on the iPhone 11, the Quick Take function lets you Tap and contain the shutter key to have a fast video as long as you're composing a normal picture. That video after that appears as a brief clip within your Photos library.

Night Mode:

This digital camera mode is immediately enabled if it is dark enough to Use it, also it works with the brand new digital camera sensors to create low-light pictures pop.

Night Mode requires shorter and much longer structures and merges them instantly for much better *low-light performance*. All **iPhone 12** versions incorporate Night time Mode on both rear and entrance cameras. The brand new *Night mode Time-Lapse function* provides longer publicity times, better lights, and smoother direct exposure for time-lapse digital photography when your cell phone is on the tripod.

Smart HDR 3:

The Wise HDR feature uses the new digital camera sensors to fully capture better HDR photos and Portrait setting shots.

ApplePro Raw:

Included in the *iPhone 12 Pro* and *iPhone 12 Pro Max*, this feature lets you capture photos in a Green format but with all the current advanced camera equipment and technologies to improve the image. You can even edit *ApplePro* Green images directly within the iPhone's Pictures app along with other third-party apps.

Design:

In a significant design change, the most recent iPhones have shifted from the curved edges from the iPhone 11 and reverted towards the flat-edged form last seen within the iPhone 5 and presently on the iPad Pro.

MagSafe:

Introduced using the **iPhone 12** lineup, **MagSafe** enhances the wireless getting built into the mobile phone for faster and much more precise getting. But there's even more. **MagSafe** offers a magnetic foundation through with add-ons can attach themselves to the mobile phone. As one instance, **Apple** provides touted a **MagSafe** suitable thin budget that attaches itself to the back of the mobile phone.

Battery:

The batteries within the **iPhone 12** versions will undoubtedly be 10% bigger than the ones within the **iPhone 11** because of the additional drain used by 5G. The **iPhone 12 Pro** and Pro Max promise at the very least an hour more of your time about the same charge, however the iPhone 12 mini's electric battery life is even more limited because of its minier size.

Colours:

The *iPhone 12 mini* and *iPhone 12* can be found in the traditional white and black but additionally blue, green, and reddish. The *iPhone 12 Pro* and *iPhone 12 Pro Max* can be purchased in blue, precious metal, graphite, and metallic.

More Features on an iPhone 12

The iPhone 12 family also contains these shared features.

- Wi-Fi 6 (802.11ax) for 38% faster download rates of speed.
- Better dirt and water level of resistance: IP68 ranking on iPhone 12 Pro for 4 meters of drinking water at around 30 minutes.
- Fast-charging to 50% battery capability in only 30 minutes.
- Audio posting with two models of Air Pods to

Beats earphones on the same iPhone.

- Spatial audio that simulates surround sound
- Dolby that simulates good motion within a 3D space
- Dual SIM with esim.

To keep straight down the costs of the brand new mobile phones and decrease the carbon footprint of accessories, Apple is selling the iPhone 12 without ear buds or charging plugs within the box. The only real accessory within the box may be the regular Charging to USB-C wire. Apple also most likely expects that lots of buyers currently have ear buds and USB chargers readily available.

What are the Different Between the Four iPhone 12 Versions?

iPhone 12 mini. The baby from the number, the iPhone 12 mini offers a display dimension of 5.4 inches with storage space choices of 64GB, 128GB, or 256GB. The display screen resolution can be 2,340 x 1,080 pixels at 476 ppi. The mobile phone includes *Ceramic Shield* in the form of a cup back and an aluminium style. The *iPhone 12 mini runs* on the dual-camera program at the back using a 12 MP wide along with a 12 MP ultra-wide zoom lens. Offered in dark, white, red, glowing blue, green, the mobile phone begins at $699.

iPhone 12. Up coming in-line, the iPhone 12 gets the most of exact same specs simply comparable to that of the iPhone 12 mini. However the iPhone 12 has a 6.1-inch screen with a resolution of 2,532 x 1,170 pixels at 460 ppi along with a beginning price of $799.

iPhone 12 Pro. The iPhone 12 Pro also offers a screen dimension of 6.1 inches with exactly the same 2,532 x 1,170 pixel quality but adds a number of sophisticated features on the iPhone 12. The device runs on the Ceramic Shield front side having a textured matte cup back and stainless design. Storage choices consist of *128GB, 256GB, and 512GB*. The three-camera program at the back provides a 12 MP telephoto zoom lens having an $f/2.0$ aperture along with a **LiDAR** scanning device. The iPhone 12 Pro also supports *Apple ProRAW* for capturing and editing pictures in Green format. This model begins at $999.

iPhone 12 Pro max. The king of bunch, the iPhone 12 Pro Max is comparable to the *iPhone 12 Pro* in most methods but supplies a screen dimension of 6.7 inches with an answer of 2,778 x 1,284 resolution at 458 ppi. The optical and electronic zoom rates may also be slightly more than those for the iPhone 12 Pro, while the cost begins at $1,099.

What are the Main Competitors of the iPhone 12?

With all iPhone 12 versions offering different sizes and functions at different costs, your competition is widely open.

iPhone 12 mini competition: Competing using the 5.4-inch iPhone 12 mini are like phones such as the Samsung *Galaxy S10e as well as the Google Pixel 4*. Beginning at $599, the Galaxy S10e supplies a 5.8-inch AMOLED screen with 2 back cameras (broad and ultra-wide), face recognition, along with a fingerprint scanner. Beginning at $799, the **Google Pixel 4** includes a 5.7-inch OLED display with wide-angle and telephoto cameras inside the back and cosmetic recognition but zero fingerprint sensor.

Neither cell phone includes *5G* connection.

iPhone 12 and 12 Pro competition: Rivals of the iPhone 12 and iPhone 12 Pro encompass many of Samsung's Galaxy cell phones, like the S10, S10 Plus, S20, and S20 FE. Among these Galaxy mobile phones, just the S20 and S20 FE are usually 5G models. Beginning at $749, the Galaxy S10 includes a 6.1-inch screen; beginning at $849, the S10 Plus bumps the display dimension to 6.4 inches. The Galaxy S20 usually begins at $999 and will be offering a 6.2-inch screen, as the S20 FE starts at only $699 using a screen sizing of 6.5 inches.

Also constructed with 5G, *Google's Pixel 5* as well as the upcoming Pixel 4A 5G are worth taking into consideration. The Google Pixel 5 begins at $699 and carries a 6-in . screen, as the Pixel 4A 5G begins at $499 and will be offering a screen dimension of 6.2 in.

iPhone 12 Pro Max competition: Competitors of the iPhone 12 Pro Max are usually Samsung's Galaxy S20 Plus, Galaxy S20 Ultra, Galaxy Notice 20, and Galaxy Note 20 Ultra. Usually beginning at $1,199, the Galaxy

S20 Plus includes a 6.7-inch screen. Beginning at $1,399, the S20 Ultra includes a whopping 6.9-inch display. The *Note 20* begins at $999 and will be offering a 6.7-inch screen, as the Note 20 Ultra starts at $1,299 and carries a 6.9-inch display.

Chapter 14

New iPhone Quick Fix

If you buy a used *iPhone mobile*, it is interesting. In the end, you would come up with an *iPhone* and stretch your budget by acquiring a used one, especially for individuals who are not economically buoyant.

Some individuals encounter this issue in their attempt of activating their new device: The new iPhone will inquire further for somebody else's **Apple ID** and wouldn't typically work unless supplied.

This isn't a challenge that can't be fixed, so; do not fret because you'll get it fixed following these steps.

- It is consequently an attribute of *Apple's Find my iPhone service* known as *Activation lock*.

- *Activation Lock* is a security measure that Apple raised to cope with the allergy of iPhone thefts. In earlier years, if someone takes an iPhone without blockage by lock feature, they could clean it, resell it, and breakout with the crime. The activation lock altered the situation.

- When the initial owner setup *finds my iPhone* on the mobile phone, the **Apple ID** used would be stored on Apple's activation servers together with almost every other information about the phone. The activation servers will most effectively unlock the phone again if that unique *Apple ID* can be used. If you no more have the *Apple ID*, you'll never be in a position to activate or use the phone. It facilitates the security of your iPhone because nobody would like to grab a phone they can't use. On the other hand, it generally does not harm you if you recently procure the phone.

- Dealing with the activation lock is annoying, but additionally, it is easy to solve. It's mainly possible, and the prior consumer just forgot to carefully turn off *find my iPhone* or erase the tool correctly before offering it on the market *(though it could also be a sign you've purchased a stolen device, so be cautious)*.

- You should contact the preceding owner of the phone for him/her to consider the necessary steps.

How to Remove Activation Lock using iCloud

Sometimes, things can get a bit messy and complicated if the merchant/seller cannot physically access the phone, thanks to circumstances such as distance, among other factors. This may also be resolved effortlessly as the owner may use iCloud to eliminate the activation lock from the phone through his accounts by following the steps below:

- Visit iCloud.com on any device, either mobile or laptop.
- Log-on with the *Apple ID* he/she used to activate the phone.
- Click *Find My iPhone.*
- Select *All Devices.*
- Go through the iPhone you sold or want to market.
- Select **Remove from Accounts.**

Having achieved that, you can pull the plug on the iPhone, and you switch it ON again. After that, you can proceed with the standard activation process.

How to Remove Activation Lock on iPhone

- It is expedient that you should unlock or remove the activation lock from the acquired iPhone by inputting the prior owners' **Apple ID.** This technique can be initiated by getting in contact with the owner and detailing the scenario.

- If the owner lives near to you, I'll recommend that you hand over the phone back to him/her with the mission to insert the mandatory unlock code, which is his/her **Apple ID**. When the seller gets the iPhone at hand, he/she only will enter the necessary *Apple ID* on the activation lock display. Having done such, restart the phone and then forge forward with the typical activation process.

How to Format an iPhone Using Find My iPhone App

This process is very much indeed identical to the approach explained above using iCloud by just using the *Find my iPhone* application installed on some other iPhone device. If the owner prefers to get this done, connect the phone you're buying to *Wi-Fi* or *mobile data*, and then inform the owner to adhere to the steps below:

- Start the *find my iPhone* app.
- Sign on with the *Apple ID* they applied to the phone sold to you.
- Choose the Phone.
- Tap *Actions*.
- Tap *Erase iPhone*.
- Tap *Erase iPhone* (It is the same button, however, on a new display).
- Enter *Apple ID*.
- Tap *Erase*.
- Tap *Remove from Accounts*.

Restart the iPhone and get started doing the setup process.

How to Wipe an iPhone Using iCloud

Imagine if you can't gain access to the *vendor/merchant* due to some reasons, yet you would need your mobile phone to be wiped entirely for easy convenience, the seller may use *iCloud* to erase it. This is attained by ensuring the phone you want to get linked to a WiFi network or mobile data network, and then inform the seller to follow along with the next steps:

- Visit https://iCloud.com/#find
- Sign in with the *Apple ID* he/she applied to the phone that is with you or sold to you.
- Click *All Devices*.
- Choose the phone sold to you or available to you.
- Select *Erase iPhone*.
- When the phone is erased, click *Remove from Accounts*.
- Restart the phone, and you are all set.

Chapter 15

Top Recommended iPhone Apps

Spark: Email App for iPhone

If you focus on *iOS apps*, you would understand that email has taken on something similar to the role of the competitor in the wonderful world of *iOS*. App designers appear to know that everyone needs a better email platform, and they want an application to resolve their issues. Controlling email is just a little less stressful if you are using **Spark** as you would find features to suit your needs, such as; sending, snoozing email messages, and a good inbox that only notifies you of important email messages.

Below are the things you'd like about this application:

- The app is simple to use and socially friendly.

- Swipe-based interaction allows for one-handed operation.

What You may not like about it:

- No filter systems for automatically sorting email messages.

- The app does not have a way of controlling messages in batches.

Things: "To-do manager" for the iPhone

To-do manager applications are a packed field, and the application called ***"Things"*** isn't the only good one, and it is also not the only *to-do manager* on this list, but it's a carefully reliable tool, seated between control and hardy. The application provides the ideal levels of both control and hardy, without mind-boggling users to dials and without dropping essential features.

Things you'd like about this application:

- This app has a simplified interface that reduces stress when adding and completing the task.

- Tasks can be added from iOS with the sheet extension.

What you may not like are:

- Repeating tasks and deadlines can be buggy.

- Tasks can't be put into the calendar automatically.

OmniCentre: GTD-compatible To-do manager App for iPhone

Like *"Things"*, *OmniCentre* is a favourite and well-designed to-do manager; however, they have a different group of priorities. Where *Things* attempts to remain simple and straightforward, *OmniCentre* is feature-rich and robust.

The application fully integrates with the *"Getting Things Done"* approach to task management called **GTD**, and this method stimulates users to jot down any duties they have, as well as almost all their associated information and scheduling. GTD users would finish up spending a great deal of time on leading and managing work; because of this, the software takes a robust feature collection to implement all areas of the GTD process.

Things you'd like about this application:

- Most effective to-do list manager available.

- Can participate in virtually any task management style.

What you may not like:

- Sacrifices simpleness and usability for power and versatility.

Agenda: iPhone App for Busy Note Takers

Agenda requires a different spin on the notes application than almost every other application; its also known as *"date centred note taking app." **Agenda*** are structured by task and day, and the times are a large part of the *Agenda*. Instead of merely collecting your jotting into a collection, *Agenda* creates a to-do list from ***"things,"*** with tight time integration, Agenda makes an operating journaling app and an able to-do manager and general iPhone note-taking app. The time and note mixture seems apparent, but *Agenda* is the first **iOS** note-taking application to perform this mixture effectively.

It's a "to-do manager" and also a note-taking application with some calendar features, which enables seeing every information in a single place with one perspective and only one app. The application is also highly practical in the freeform, which may be uncommon in flagship apps. The beauty of the app *"Agenda"* comes out when using Pencil support, but for the present time, we'll have to turn to the *iPad Pro* for the feature.

Things you'd like about this application:

- Note-taking small tweaks can improve many workflows.
- The time-based organization fits most users; mental types of information organization.

What you may not like:

- Slow app release can limit how quickly you can write down a note.

1Password: iPhone App for Security Password Management

Using the auto-fill in *iOS 14*, *1Password* is as near to perfect as we have in a password manager. The *Face ID* authentication isn't unique to the iPhone 12 alone, but access *Face ID* makes the application better and simpler to use, which is an uncommon combination of accomplishments to reach concurrently.

Things you'd like about this application:

- Finding and copying usernames and passwords is extremely easy.

- Secure document storage space means *1Password* can gather all of your secure information in a single place.

- Auto-fill support finally makes security password management as easy as typing your security password.

What you may not like:

- No **Free** version.

- The paid version uses membership pricing.

Twitterific: Tweets App for iPhone

Twitter is probably not the most exceptional social media system, but it's still one of the very most popular internet sites around, and like many internet sites, Twitter's default application is disappointingly bad.

Unfortunately, Twitter does lately nerf third-party Twitter clients. Third-party applications won't receive real-time stream notifications, significantly reducing the effectiveness of the applications; this move seems to pressure users to go to the native app, but considering its many defects, *Twitterific* and applications like it remain better.

Things you'd like about this application:

- Improves Twitter's visual effects dramatically.

- Includes smart and powerful features that make Twitter simpler to use.

What you may not like:

- Some organizational options are initially unintuitive.

- Twitter has purposefully knee-capped a good

number of third-party apps, and *Twitterific* is no defence to those results.

Overcast: iPhone App for Podcasts

Overcast is the best application you may use to listen to *podcasts*. The app's user interface is considered carefully for *maximal consumer performance*, with features like *"Smart Time"* which helps to intelligently manage a podcast's playback speed to shorten silences without accelerating speech, while Tone of voice Boost offers a pre-built *EQ* curve made to amplify voices, which is ideal for a loud hearing environment.

Things you'd like about this application:

- Thoughtfully designed interface for sorting and hearing podcasts.

- Features like Smart Speed and Queue playlists are invaluable once you're used to them.

- Active developer centred on avoiding an unhealthy user experience on monetization.

What you may not like;

- It most definitely doesn't seem to go nicely with the iOS lock screen.

Apollo: iPhone App for Reddit

If you're thinking about *Reddit*, you would want to see the website beyond the third-party app. The application has improved, sure, but it's still kilometres behind third-party offerings.

Apollo is the best of the number as it pertains to *Reddit clients*, conquering out past champions like "Narwhal." Development is continuous and ongoing, with many improvements from the dev in the app's subreddit.

The swipe-based navigation would continue to work on any iPhone, of course, but it dovetails nicely with the iPhone application switching behaviour. The real black setting is also a delicacy for *OLED* screens.

Things you'd like about this application:

- Effortlessly handles an enormous variety of media.

- Well developed *UI* makes navigation easy.

- No ads in virtually any version of the app.

What you may not like:

- Sometimes is suffering from annoying and lingering bugs.

<u>Focos</u>: iPhone App for Editing and Enhancing Portrait Setting Photos

By default, the iPhone *Portrait Mode* is a one-and-done process; you take the picture, and the blur is applied. iOS doesn't give a built-in way for editing and enhancing the Picture Setting effect following the fact. **Focos** fills the space, creating a tool to tweak both degrees of shadow and the blur face mask. It mimics the result you'd see when modifying a zoom lens' physical aperture. More magically, you can also change the centre point following the shot by recreating the blurred cover up on the different object, or by hand adjusting the result on the image's depth face mask instantly.

Things you'd like about this application:

- The most effective approach to manipulating Portrait Mode's depth-of-field effect.

- The depth field is a distinctive feature to help visualize blur.

What you may not like:

- Simple to make images look over-processed.

- Only about the centre, *50%* of the blur range looks natural.

Halide: iPhone App for Natural Photos

Distinctively, *Halide* sticks essential info in the iPhone "ear." It embeds a live histogram for image evaluation; could it be precious? Nearly, but *Halide* is a near-perfect picture taking software besides that offering feature.

The settings are ideally positioned and configured, the

RAW catch is *pixel-perfect*, and navigation within the application is easy and immediately understandable. If you are seriously interested in taking photos on your iPhone, *Halide* is the best camera application for iOS.

Things you'd like about this application:

- Low handling power for iPhone photos.

- The broadest toolset of any iOS image editing and enhancing the app.

What you may not like:

- It can overwhelm first-time users using its degree of control.

Euclidean Lands: AR Puzzle Game for iPhone

Augmented reality applications haven't yet found their killer use. But *AR* gambling takes great benefit from lots of the iPhone features.

Euclidean Lands is a short fun puzzler that calls for the full benefit of AR's potential. Similar to *Monument*

Valley, players manipulate the play space to produce new pathways through puzzle designs, guiding their avatar to the finish of the maze. The overall game begins easy; nevertheless, you might be scratching your head just a little by the end.

Things you'd like in this application:

- Challenging and attractive puzzle levels that take benefit of AR's unique features.

What you may not like:

- Disappointingly short.

- The core game auto technician feels very familiar.

Giphy World: AR Messaging App for iPhone

Plenty of applications have tried to usurp *Snapchat* as an *AR* messaging system. While Snapchat might maintain a weakened condition because of self-inflicted damage, it isn't eliminated yet. But if it can decrease, *Giphy World* is a great replacement.

Things you'd like about this application:

- Simple to create fun and funny images from provided assets.

- Content isn't locked inside the *Giphy app.*

What you may not like:

- Object place and processing speed are inferior compared to Snapchat's.

Jig Space: AR for Education on iPhone

Learning with *holograms* is one particular thing you regularly see in sci-fi movies; with **Jig Space** and **augmented** actuality, that kind of thing is now possible in our daily lives. You should use the application to find out about various topics, including what sort of lock works, manipulating every part of the system, and looking at it from alternative perspectives. Jig Space requires the benefit of AR's three sizes effectively, and the low-poly models AR has bound not to harm the grade of the visualizations.

Things you'd like about this application:

- Takes benefit of AR's advantages for a good cause.

- A substantial assortment of *"jigs"* charges is free.

What you may not like:

- Accompanying captions are occasionally disappointingly shallow.

Nighttime Sky: Night Companion App

Directing out constellations is much more fun if you are not making them up as you decide to go. *Evening Sky* was the main augmented-reality style application to see on iOS. It shows just how far others on the system wanting to mimic its success, but it remained dominant nevertheless.

Things you'd like about this application:

- It enhances the natural world with technology.

- It improves the star-gazing experience for both

children and adults.

What you may not like:

- Large image units mean large camera motions are stiff and jerky.

Inkhunter: Readily Useful AR Gimmick on iOS

There's something distinctively exotic about checking out new tattoos by yourself. *Inkhunter* uses the energy of augmented truth to generate short-term digital symbols you can construct on the body and screenshot. You should use the built-in adobe flash, pull your designs, or import project from somewhere else to project on your skin.

Things you'd like about this application:

- Fun and book application idea that's useful.

What you may not like:

- is suffering from AR's existing restrictions in surface matching.

Chapter 16

How to Format iPhone 12

We shall give some instructions below to format iPhone 12 operating-system to manufacturing default. Please be aware, these options might not work if various other troubles occur on your iPhone.

Hard Reset iPhone 12 with Software Program Menu:

- Make certain the battery will be charged rightly
- Turn on *iPhone 12.*
- Don't forget to backup almost all important information, please use *iTunes* for *quick backup and restore.*
- Go to menu: *Setting > General.*
- At the *General menu page*, please head to the bottom part and choose *Reset.*
- Choose to *Erase all Content and Settings* to keep reformat or hard reset *iPhone 12.*
- Please wait for several moments until prepared to use in clear factory default.

Hard Reset iPhone 12 with iTune Software From Pc (This Options also work For Back-Up & Restore with iTunes):

- Download and prepare installed *iTune programs* on PC (*MacOS* or even *Microsoft Home windows*)

- Start iTunes on your personal computer, after iTunes set, connect to *iPhone USB Cable*

- On *iTunes*, you must choose the iPhone. We can also click **Gadget** if our iTunes show up on the sidebar

- You can carry out *Backup* or even *Restore* as of these steps

- Make sure you choose *Restore*

- You will have the *Software program update windows*

- If you notice a software license contract, choose *Agree*

- Please wait whilst iPhone get the manufacturer to default operating-system reinstall or even restore until iTunes will display *"Welcome to Your Brand-New iPhone"*

- If you want to use the new *iPhone 12*, then choose *Setup a brand-new iPhone*

- If you want to restore all backup information to *iPhone 12*, then choose *Restore*

How to Restore and Reinstall, Clear iOS/Firmware on iPhone 12

Under normal circumstances, the iOS is quite stable functioning on your iPhone 12. Nevertheless, some issue takes place with application accident that produces iOS harm. You have to reformat or reinstall stock default iOS. Firstly; you must understand that iOS document source already stored safely in *iPhone 12 Rom or memory*, consequently, you need not copy from some other gadget unless reformat, making use of iTunes to back-up and restore all information as well. Make sure you follow one to adhere to steps to hard reset or reformat above, after that, clean manufacturing default iOS firmware or operating-system will undoubtedly be reinstalled automatically.

How to Unlock or Fix or Bypass Forgoten Security Password

iPhone has quite strong information protections whenever we make use of screen lock protection. You can safely have your essential or confidential information secure when your *iPhone 12* is dropped or taken or stolen. The issues happen whenever You forgot what's the security password pin or security password.

How exactly can you unlock or bypass forgot safety protection or security password pin on iPhone 12?

You must reinstall or restore use of *iTunes*, additionally; you must hard reset and clear all important information, please follow methods to hard reset by making use of *iTunes* as previously explained in this book, but if you've currently backup some information, You can restore it again after yo are done with reinstalling or hard resetting of your iPhone 12.

How to Back-up and Restore Data on iPhone 12

You can back-up and restore all important information

and installed programs, also device menu using *iTunes* which you have to install on your MacOS device or even using Personal computer (Microsoft Windows Operating System). Please follow ways to hard reset your phone as discussed earlier, after that run the procedure to back-up and restore.

How to Update iOS at iPhone 12

You can up-date anytime you wish using *OTA* or even using *iTunes* for the most recent version of *iOS*.

How do you enter Accessibility mode on iPhone 12 and 12 Pro!

Unlike other gestures, you need to do need to arrange it first.

- Launch *Settings* from the *home screen*.
- Tap on *general*.
- Tap on *accessibility*.
- Toggle accessibility to *On*.

Once setup:

- Tap your finger on the gesture area at the bottom of the *iPhone 12 screen*.

- Swipe down.

You can also swipe down from the top right of accessibility to access *Control Center*.

Chapter 17

iPhone Tips & Tricks

How to Enable USB Restricted Setting on iPhone

Apple just built a robust new security feature into the iPhone with the latest version of iOS; this launch is what's known as *USB Restricted Setting* on the iPhone. Lately, companies have been making devices that may be connected to an iPhone's USB slot and crack an iPhone's passcode.

To protect from this, Apple has introduced a USB Restricted Setting. USB Restricted Setting disabled data writing between an iPhone and a USB device if the iPhone is not unlocked to get more than one hour; this effectively makes the iPhone breaking boxes ineffective as they may take hours or times to unlock a locked iPhone.

By default, *USB Restricted Mode* is enabled in iOS. But for those who want to disable it, or make sure it hasn't been disabled, go to the *Configurations app* and touch

Face ID & Passcode. Enter your passcode and then swipe down until you visit a section entitled ***"Allow Access When Locked."***

The final toggle in this section is a field that says *"USB Accessories. "* The toggle next to them should be turned OFF (white); this implies *USB Restricted Setting* is allowed, and devices can't download or upload data from/to your iPhone if the iPhone is not unlocked to get more than one hour.

Control Your Apple TV with Your iPhone

The Control Focus on the iPhone has an impressive trick: it enables you to regulate your Apple TV if you have one. As long as your iPhone and Apple TV are on a single mobile network, it'll work. Get into Control Centre and then look for the Apple TV button that shows up. Touch it and start managing your Apple TV.

Use Two Pane Scenery View

This tip only pertains to the iPhone 11 Pro Max but is cool nonetheless. If you have your iPhone XS device horizontally when using specific applications, you'll see lots of the built-in apps changes to a two-pane setting, including Email and Records. This setting is the main one you observe on an iPad where, for example, you can see a list of all of your note in the Records app while positively reading or editing a single note.

How to stop iPhone Alarms with Your Face

An extremely cool feature of the iPhone is Face ID. It gives you to unlock your phone just by taking a look at it. *Face ID* also has various other cool features-like that one. Whenever your iPhone security alarm goes off, you could silent it by just picking right up your iPhone and taking a look at it; this tells your iPhone you understand about the arm, and it'll quiet it.

Quickly Disable Face ID

Depending on your geographical area, the police might be able to legally demand you uncover your smartphone at that moment via its facial recognition features. For reasons unknown, facial biometrics aren't protected in the manner fingerprints, and passcodes are; in a few localities. That's why Apple has generated an attribute that lets you quickly disable *Face ID* in a pinch without going into your settings. Just press the side button five times, and *Face ID* will be disabled, and you'll need to enter your passcode instead to gain access to your phone.

How to Slow the two times click necessary for Apple Pay

Given that the iPhone jettisoned the *Touch ID* sensor, you confirm your **Apple Pay** obligations by using *Face ID* and twice pressing the medial side button. By default, you would need to dual press the medial side button pretty quickly-but it is possible to make things slow down.

To take action, go to *Settings > General > Availability*. Now scroll right down to Side Button. Privately Button screen, you can select between *default, gradual, or slowest*. Pick the speed that is most effective for you.

Chapter 18

iPhone 12 Problems & the Solution

As we drive away from the discharge of Apple's *iPhone 12* and *iPhone 12 Pro* we're hearing concerning the issues plaguing both flagship models.

The *iPhone 12* and *iPhone 12 Pro* have already been out for a couple weeks this means we're getting feedback from early adopters.

Most of the comments continues to be good, but we've also found out about a number of performance issues and bugs plaguing both phones.

Luckily, there's a good opportunity you'll have the ability to fix your ailing phone prior to new software program arrives or just before you're forced to get contacting the *Apple customer care.*

In this section we'll take you through fixes for a few of the very most common *iPhone 12 and iPhone 12 Pro problems.* The listing consists of fixes for *Wi-Fi problems, fixes for Bluetooth difficulties, fixes for getting issues, and much more.*

How to Repair iPhone 12 Battery Life

Many iPhone 12 and iPhone 12 Pro users are usually enjoying excellent electric battery life. Nevertheless, some are beginning to notice the electric battery drain quicker than its expected.

In case your **iPhone 12** or **iPhone 12 Pro's** battery life starts draining faster than it will, there are a few steps you need to take before contacting **Apple** support.

Using the **iPhone 12** and **iPhone 12 Pro** now in the hands of users all over the world, we would need to get feedback about their performance.

Most of the suggestions continues to be great. Nevertheless, we're also listening to about a selection of problems owners of the brand new 6.1-inch choices are coping with.

We haven't seen widespread issues about battery existence (*not yet at the very least*), however, many users say their electric battery is draining faster than it ought to be.

Battery life problems are normal (particularly after Apple releases brand-new **iOS** software program) and we realize that **5G** drain batteries faster than **LTE** so these complaints aren't amazing.

If you begin noticing severe electric battery drain, there are a few actions you can take to resolve the problem. In ths section of the book we'll get you through some fixes that may help you repair poor iPhone 12 electric battery life.

They are fixes which have worked for all of us over time and they will help you solve your electric battery issues in moments and assist you to avoid a talk session with *Apple customer support.*

Restart Your Phone

In case your battery starts draining faster than you imagine it will, we always recommend restarting your cell phone before doing other things.

Power your *iPhone 12/iPhone 12 Pro* down, wait one minute, and power it ON again. If it's nevertheless draining quickly, move ahead to these some other steps.

Up-date Your iPhone

Apple periodically produces software updates for the iPhone. Point up-dates (x.x.x) are usually focused on mending bugs whilst milestone improvements (x.x) usually deliver a variety of functions and fixes.

The company may not call out battery lifestyle fixes within an iOS update's change log, but new *firmware* always gets the potential to greatly help alleviate battery issues.

Switch Off 5G

The **iPhone 12** and **iPhone 12 Pro** both assistance **5G** connectivity. While quick, it might drain your electric battery considerably faster than **LTE** will. If you don't have to make use of 5G or you don't have to use it on a regular basis, go to your *iPhone 12's configurations.*

iOS 14 includes a couple of 5G configurations that you'll desire to invest in as your memory lender. To get these you'll need to head into Configurations, then Cellular, after that Cellular Data Choices, then Tone of voice & Data.

If you're in the right place you'll see three options:

- *5G On*
- *5G Auto*
- *LTE*

5G On means that your iPhone use 5G whenever it's obtainable, even if it might get rid of your device's electric battery life.

The *5G Auto* option only uses 5G only once it won't significantly deplete your phone's battery. *5G Auto* may be the default and the choice a lot of people should select.

Examine Your Apps

Apps will often have a poor effect on your phone's electric battery length and you'll need to consider them if you're noticing abnormal drain.

Checking app performance is incredibly easy on the *iPhone 12/iPhone 12 Pro*. Here's how exactly to do it:

- Go to your *Settings app.*
- Select *Battery.*
- Scroll right down to the *Battery Utilization tool.*

This battery use tool teaches you the apps draining your iPhone 12's battery when they're doing this.

If you are using an app a whole lot, it'll obviously drain even more electric battery than apps you won't ever use. If you observe an app you hardly ever make use of sucking up a huge amount of power, you'll need to investigate further.

If you notice an app sucking up a huge amount of battery lifetime, try deleting the app from your device and find out if the condition has improved.

If the app is vital to your day-to-day use, we recommend downloading the most recent update from your developer. If that doesn't assist, and you actually need the app to do your daiy activities, you may need to downgrade back to a previous edition of iOS 14.

Reset All Settings

Before you do that, note that it'll cause your device to forget known Wi-Fi networks therefore be sure you have your passwords on paper or stored someplace before you do that.

- Head to *Settings*.
- Go to *General*.
- Scroll and tap *Reset*.
- Tap *Reset All Settings* and enter your pass code if the first is enabled.

Once the course of action is complete, you'll have to reconnect your iPhone to your Wi-Fi system(s) and Bluetooth devices.

Use Low Power Mode

iOS 14's *Lower Power Mode* can help you preserve battery life by shutting off solutions (*Hey Siri, auto downloads, and email fetch*) which could drain your battery.

It is possible to turn *Low Power Setting On/Off* if you want as well as the operating system may also prompt you to carefully turn it On when your iPhone reaches 20% battery.

If you haven't done thus already, add *Low Power Mode* to your *Control Center*. Control Center may be the menus that arises once you swipe up from underneath or, if you're utilizing a newer iPhone model, from the top right of the display. Here's how to do this:

- Head to *Settings*
- Tap *Control center.*
- Tap *Customize Settings.*
- Tap the *green (+) plus* sign close to *Low Power Setting.*

Next time you start *Control Center* on your phone you'll see a battery icon. Touch it make it possible for, or disable, *Lower Power Mode* on your device.

You can even turn *Low Power Setting* On via your *Settings*. Here's how exactly to do this:

- Head to *Settings*.
- Tap *Battery*.
- Tap *Low Power Mode.*
- Toggle it *On.*

Stop Background Rebrand-new

Background Rebrand-new apps inside the background to

be able to show you the most recent data once you open them up. It's a good feature, nonetheless it can also consume electric battery life. If you don't require it, attempt switching it off. Here's how exactly to do this:

- Head to *Settings*.
- Tap *General.*
- Tap *Background App Rebrand-new.*
- Turn it Off, and any applications you don't make use of.

You can even turn it completely off if you don't desire to proceed through your apps individually.

Downgrade

If you can't look for a fix for the issue, and/or don't desire to await Apple's next *iOS 14 update*, you can test downgrading your *iPhone 12's* software program (if the choice can be acquired).

How to Repair iPhone 12 Missing 5G

If you simply opened your brand-new iPhone 12 or iPhone 12 Pro you're probably thinking about making use of your carrier's 5G system. The iPhone 12 and iPhone 12 Pro are the first iPhones with 5G connection. That said, you should be on an idea that helps 5G connectivity.

If you go into the Cellular portion of your phone's *Settings app* and you also don't see any choices for 5G, this isn't a bug. It's most likely because you're not currently on the 5G-allowed plan together with your provider. If that's the situation, you'll only observe *"LTE"* and *"4G."*

To make use of your carrier's **5G** network you'll likely have to switch/upgrade your strategy. Before you decide to do so, make certain 5G service comes in the places you frequently use. You can do that via the service provider 5G maps below:

- *AT&T 5G Map*
- *T-Mobile 5G Map*

- *Sprint 5G Map*
- *Verizon 5G Map*

One other note: If you personally have an *AT&T iPhone 12 or iPhone 12 Pro*, you might observe that your phone is linked to 5G when its not linked to **Wi-Fi**. This isn't *AT&T's 5G system*.

5G means 5G Development and it's a rebranding from the carrier's *LTE-A support*.

How to Repair iPhone 12 Wi-Fi Problems

If you begin noticing slow *Wi-Fi* rates of speed or a rise in dropped contacts, below are a few things you can test before getting back in connection with customer service.

Before you begin fiddling with your iPhone 12's settings, you'll desire to investigate the *Wi-Fi* connection providing you problems. If you're on your home Wi-Fi system, attempt unplugging the router for a moment before plugging it back in.

If you're good it's not the router, you might like to check and find out if other people with the same ISP are experiencing similar issues locally.

If you can't access the router your cell phone is linked to or if you're good, the problem has nothing to do with connection with your ISP/router, go to your iPhone 12's *Settings app*.

Once you're here, you'll need to check Wi-Fi system if you're having problems. Here's how exactly to do this:

- In Settings, tap *Wi-Fi*.

- Choose your connection by tapping the *"i"* in the circle.

- Tap *Forget this Network* near the top of the display. (**Note:** *This can trigger your iPhone the request for your Wi-Fi password.*)

If this doesn't function, try resetting your iPhone's system settings:

- Head to your *Settings app*.

- Tap *General*.

- Tap *Reset*

- Tap on *Reset Network Settings*.

How to Repair iPhone 12 Bluetooth Problems

In case your *iPhone 12* or *iPhone 12 Pro* struggles to connect to a number of one's Bluetooth devices, there are many steps to take.

One thing you'll wish to accomplish is your *Bluetooth connection* that's giving you issues. Here's how exactly to do this:

- Go to the *Settings app*.
- Tap *Bluetooth*.
- Choose the connection utilizing the *"i"* within the circle
- Tap *"Forget this device"*.
- Try reconnecting to the *Bluetooth* device.

If that doesn't function, you should attempt resetting your Network Configurations:

- Head to your *Settings*.
- Tap *General*.
- Tap *Reset*.
- Tap *Reset System Settings*.

This process will need a couple of seconds to accomplish. It will result in your iPhone neglecting known Wi-Fi systems, so make certain you've got your security password(s) handy.

You can even try resetting your device's settings back to their factory defaults, though this will only be achieved as a final resort. Here's how exactly to do this:

- Go to the *Settings app.*
- Tap *General.*
- Tap *Reset.*
- Tap *Reset All Settings.*

If none of these fixes work, you likely have to get hold of Apple's customer support or if it's no Apple item, the company which makes the Bluetooth item you're attempting to connect to.

How to Repair iPhone 12 Charging Faults

We've observed some issues about iPhone 12 getting issues & most of the issues has to do with the *wifi charging feature.*

If you experience a concern with wireless charging, reset your iPhone. To get this done, press and launch *Volume up*, push and release *volume down*, and hold down the *power button* before the cell phone *turns off*. Change the device back if the feature is operating normally.

If you're utilizing an iphone cover to store bank cards or security, you'll need to remove those before charging your phone. Additionally, you might try getting your device off and attempt charging your mobile phone that way.

How to Repair iPhone 12 Cell Network Problems

In case your iPhone suddenly displays a *"Simply no Service"* symbol and you also can't hook up to your cellular network, here are some steps to take.

First, make certain presently there isn't an outage locally. Check social media for reviews and/or enter connection with your company on social media. You can even check out network signal and find out if others locally are having comparable issues.

If you observe that the problem is unrelated to some system outage, you'll need to restart your iPhone and find out if that fixes the problem.

If that doesn't work, try turning **Airplane Setting On** for 30 seconds before switching it **Off.**

If you now can't get it to operate normally, you'll need to try shutting off Cellular Data completely. To achieve that, here's what you ought to do:

- Head to *Settings*.
- Tap *Cellular.*
- Toggle *Cellular Information* to *Off.*
- Turn it *Off* for one minute and toggle it back.

How to Repair iPhone 12 Sound Problems

Your iPhone 12's speakers should provide loud, sharp audio. However, in case your audio begins to crackle or audio muffled, here are some things you can test before getting back in contact with *Apple customer service.*

Firstly; restart your iPhone. Additionally, you should check to be sure your SIM card is positioned rightly in the holder. The SIM card slot on the iPhone 12 is situated on the remaining side of the mobile phone.

You can even try turning *Bluetooth connectivity On/Off.*

If the sound from the mobile phone continues to be missing or distorted, make certain there aren't particles blocking the loudspeaker grille or the Lightning slot.

If you begin noticing an abrupt drop in contact high quality, restart your cell phone. You'll also need to check out the device's recipient to be sure it's not blocked by particles or your display screen protector when you have one. You can even try eliminating your situation if you're making use of one to find out if that helps.

In case your phone's mic suddenly stops functioning or starts arbitrarily eliminating, try restarting your mobile phone.

If the mic continues to be busted, you can test restoring your phone from the backup. If repairing doesn't function, you'll need to get contact of Apple as you may have a hardware problem.

How to Repair iPhone 12 Activation Problems

If you're setting your iPhone 12 or iPhone 12 Pro and you're struggling to activate it rightly, here are some things you can test.

First, make certain Apple's systems are usually ready to go. You can certainly do that over right here within the company's Program Status page. If you notice green close to *iOS device Activation*, Apple's solutions should be functioning normally.

If you visit a natural symbol but still can't activate it, ensure that your SIM credit card is rightly inserted within your iPhone. Furthermore, make certain you're utilizing the correct SIM credit card.

If you're viewing an alert that states *Invalid SIM or Zero SIM*, and you're good, you're utilizing the correct SIM cards, here are some additional actions to get:

- Be sure you have an active plan with your wireless carrier.
- Update your iPhone to the most recent edition of iOS.
- Restart your phone.

- Check for the carrier settings update. Go into *Configurations > Common > About*. If an upgrade can be acquired, you'll see a prompt to choose **OK** or **Up-date**.

If none of these work, contact **Apple** or your provider company.

How to Repair iPhone 12 Performance

In case your iPhone 12 or iPhone 12 Pro is lagging, freezing, or locking up, or you come across another performance issue, please have a look at the set of fixes for performance issues.

As we push from the **iOS 14.1** launch date we're listening to several issues including several performance issues impacting iPhone choices.

While most of the comments about iOS 14.1 continue to be good, we've been using a good Face across the majority of our products, we've been hearing about bugs and performance problems.

The current listing includes *UI lag, freezes, lock-ups, and random reboots*. They are incredibly common, especially on old iPhone versions. Newer iPhones aren't immune in their form though.

Unfortunately, performance problems such as these could be tricky to repair. However, you might have the ability to repair them by yourself, some may need a repair from Apple in a brand-new software update.

If you can't wait and/or you don't have time and energy to speak to Apple support, we've some fixes which could help alleviate the overall performance issue(s) you're seeing on your device.

Restart Your iPhone

If you begin noticing *UI lag* or another efficiency issue on your iPhone, *try restarting it*. When the power is down, keep it off for one minute, as well as turn it back on.

Up-date Your iPhone

Apple may periodically discharge the new iOS 14 software program. Point up-dates (x.x.x) are often focused on mending bugs whilst milestone improvements (x.x) usually deliver a variety of functions and fixes.

Update Your App

App developers are rolling out iOS 14 assistance updates plus they may help stabilize iOS 14's overall performance on your device.

Before you decide to install the most recent version make sure to go into the App Store and go through critiques/reviews from other iOS 14/iOS 14.1 customers. When the evaluations are mainly good, you'll need to download the most recent version.

Reset Your Settings

If you're even not obtaining the kind of efficiency you need, try resetting your iPhone's configurations. Here's how exactly to do this on iOS 14:

- Head to *Settings.*
- Tap *General.*
- Tap *Reset.*
- Tap *Reset All Settings.*
- Enter your *passcode* if you have one enabled.

This can restore your iPhone's settings with their factory defaults so make sure to have your Wi-Fi passwords handy. You'll have to re-enter them.

Cleanup Your Storage

If you've had your iPhone for quite some time there's an extreme opportunity you've got plenty of clutter taking on the area on its internal storage space. Deleting this mess could help increase your iPhone.

To start, you'll need to check out and observe how very much space is free of charge on your device. Here's how exactly to do this:

- Go to *Settings.*
- Tap *General.*
- Tap *Storage space & iCloud Usage.*
- Select *Manage Storage Space.*

If you're approaching the threshold you'll need to return into General and scroll to where it says *iPhone Storage space*. Here you'll get yourself a complete rundown of one's data.

Apple can make some suggestions predicated on the use of your storage space, but you may also just proceed through each area manually to delete documents you don't want.

Stop Auto Downloads

iOS's automatic update feature can be handy, but a continuing stream of updates can make your iPhone function in the background.

If you're alright with manually updating your programs on the App Store, try disabling *Auto Downloads* on your iPhone and find out if performance improves a little.

To get this done you'll go to *Settings*. Following that, *Touch iTunes & App Store*. Following that you'll need to toggle Up-dates, situated in the Auto Downloads area, off. You might like to toggle other options off aswell.

Disable Widgets

iOS 14 brought quite a few big style upgrades to Widgets. That said, if you don't make use of Widgets on your iPhone, attempt disabling some or them all to find out if that helps.

To achieve that, you'll need to swipe to the right while you're on your iPhone's home display. After that, you might have two choices. It is possible to:

- *Hard press* on the *Widget*
- Scroll completely to the bottom of the screen and

choose *Edit*. This can lead them to start wiggling.

If you hard press on the *Widget*, a little menus will popup. To eliminate a widget you'll need to tap on *Delete Widget* at the very top.

If you selected *Edit* at the bottom, you can Tap the minus to remain a wiggling Widget to eliminate it. You can even scroll right down to underneath and choose *Customize*. This can enable you to quickly include or remove *Widgets*.

We recommend disabling *Widgets* you don't use. Keep in mind, you can turn them back On if you don't see a bump in functionality.

Clear Internet Browser Cookies & Data

Clearing your browser's cookies and data will release memory that could have a confident effect on your phone's performance.

If you are using *Apple's Internet browser* go into the *Settings app*, touch *Browser*, and scroll right down to where it states *Clear Background* and *Website Data*. Tap on it.

Tapping this can remove your searching Background,

cookies, along other data from Browser. The background may also be cleared from any gadgets signed into the *iCloud accounts*. If you're good with that, Tap *Clear Background and Data again.*

If you are using *Google Chrome*, you'll need to go to the app and touch the three horizontal circles underneath the right part. They're in the very best right corner if you haven't updated with *Chrome's brand-new features*.

Once there, *Tap Settings*, tap *Personal privacy*, and now touch *Clear Browsing Cookies*. Now you can select everything you need to delete. If you're experiencing heavy lag, you might like to clear everything.

Stop Using Background Rebrand-new

iOS 14's Background App Rebrand-new apps works in the background by showing you the most recent data when you open up them up. Besides, it makes your cell phone work in the background if you don't want this, you might like to shut it off.

Here's the method that you need to disable it:

- Go into the *Settings app.*
- Tap *General.*

- Tap *Background App Rebrand-new*.

- At the very top tap *Background App Rebrand-new* and *toggle it off*.

If you wish to keep it on for a few apps, keep it on and decrease your set of apps and manually turn it off for apps you don't use.

How to Repair iPhone 12 Face ID Problems

If you're having problems with your phone's **Face ID** feature, here are some things you can test.

First, ensure that your iPhone 12 is working on the most recent version of *iOS*.

If you're operating the most recent version of iOS 14 and you're looking at issues, go to the *Face ID settings*.

- Head to *Settings*.

- Head into *Face ID & Passcode*. Remember that you'll need to enter your passcode (when you have one) to get access.

Once you're within, ensure that *Face ID* is set up on your mobile phone and that the functions you're attempting to make use of *Face ID* with are turned On.

If you're having issues making use of your Face to unlock your cell phone, make certain you're actively considering the screen.

If you are constantly modifying your appearance, you may want to include another appearance to *Face ID*. To create an alternate look, here's what you ought to do:

- Head to *Settings*.
- Tap *Face ID & Passcode*.
- Tap *Setup an Alternate Look*.

You'll also need to make certain there aren't any particles (dirt, etc) blocking your iPhone 12's front-facing digital camera.

If your gadget isn't registering that Face when you're establishing a *Face ID*, make certain you're scanning it in a well-lit space. You also may need to provide the *iPhone 12* nearer to that person or take it, leveler.

How to Repair iPhone 12 Overheating Problems

We've seen the reviews about *iPhone 12/iPhone 12 Pro* models working hot through the setup even though operating apps and providers like *GPS*. If you don't need to get your phone right into a store, here are some things to try out.

Very first, try removing the affected app (if you're using one) and find out if that assists. You'll also need to attempt turning the mobile phone Off and On. You can even try putting the mobile phone into *Airplane Setting*.

INDEX

CPSIA information can be obtained
at www.ICGtesting.com
Printed in the USA
LVHW082318210521
687963LV00002B/7